NORMAL LOAN

Remember to return on time **or** renew at
https://icity.bcu.ac.uk/ or
http://www0.bcu.ac.uk/library/public/
or **24 Hour Renewals: Tel 0121 331 5278**
Items in demand may not be renewable

FEB

MAR 9

992

Communications and Culture

Communications has been defined as the conveying or exchanging of information and ideas. This wide definition is taken as the starting-point for this series of books, which are not bound by conventional academic divisions. The series aims to document or analyse a broad range of cultural forms and ideas.

It encompasses works from areas as esoteric as linguistics and as exoteric as television. The language of communication may be the written word or the moving picture, the static icon or the living gesture. These means of communicating can at their best blossom into and form an essential part of the other mysterious concept, *culture*.

There is no sharp or intended split in the series between communication and culture. On one definition, culture refers to the organisation of experience shared by members of a community, a process which includes the standards and values for judging or perceiving, for predicting and acting. In this sense, creative communication can make for a better and livelier culture.

The series reaches towards the widest possible audience. Some of the works concern themselves with activities as general as play and games; others offer a narrower focus, such as the ways of understanding the visual image. It is hoped that some moves in the transformation of the artful and the scientific can be achieved, and that both can begin to be understood by a wider and more comprehending community. Some of these books are written by practitioners – broadcasters, journalists, and artists; others come from critics, scholars, scientists and historians.

The series has an ancient and laudable, though perhaps untenable, aim – an aim as old as the Greeks and as new as holography: it aspires to help heal the split between cultures, between the practitioners and the thinkers, between science and art, between the academy and life.

PAUL WALTON

COMMUNICATIONS AND CULTURE

Editorial Board PHILIP CORRIGAN, STUART HALL, RICHARD HOGGART, STUART HOOD, ANTHONY SMITH, PAUL WALTON AND RAYMOND WILLIAMS

Published

James Curran (ed.) THE BRITISH PRESS: A MANIFESTO

Carl Gardner (ed.) MEDIA, POLITICS AND CULTURE: A SOCIALIST VIEW

Erving Goffman GENDER ADVERTISEMENTS

Anthony Smith THE POLITICS OF INFORMATION: PROBLEMS OF POLICY IN MODERN MEDIA

Forthcoming

Stuart Hall REPRODUCING IDEOLOGIES

Stephen Heath FILM THEORY

Herbert Marcuse THE AESTHETIC DIMENSION

Dipak Nandy BROADCASTING AND THE PUBLIC INTEREST

Michael Tracey and David Morrison THE SECULAR CRUSADE OF MARY WHITEHOUSE

Michael Tracey and David Morrison MARY WHITEHOUSE AND THE N.V.A.L.A.

Brian Winston and Colin Young FILM

Keith Yeomans, Sarah Lovegrove and John Brown LOCAL RADIO: DEVELOPMENTS, ACCESS AND CONTROL

Jock Young MEDIA AS MYTH

Media, Politics and Culture

A Socialist View

Edited by

CARL GARDNER

M

First published 1979 by
THE MACMILLAN PRESS LTD
London and Basingstoke
Associated companies in Delhi Dublin
Hong Kong Johannesburg Lagos Melbourne
New York Singapore and Tokyo

Printed in Great Britain by
LOWE AND BRYDONE PRINTERS LTD
Thetford, Norfolk

British Library Cataloguing in Publication Data

Media, politics and culture. – (Communications and culture).
  1. Mass media – Great Britain
  I. Gardner, Carl II. Series
  301.16′1′0941   P92.G7

  ISBN 0–333–23588–6
  ISBN 0–333–23589–4 Pbk

This book is dedicated to the memory of Martin
Walsh (1947–77), with whom I would have dearly
loved to discuss it.

Contents

Acknowledgements

In addition to all the contributors, I would like to thank Malcolm Imrie, for undertaking the tedious job of transcription; Andrew de la Tour, for being instrumental in organising the original discussion—series from which the present volume emerged; and Mike Chanan, for help in compiling the bibliography.

Introduction

Carl Gardner

This collection of essays originated in autumn 1976, when members of the National Union of Journalists and Equity in the International Marxist Group decided to hold a series of open public forums in London on the mass media. The motivation for this series was confused, but as the publicity material stated:

> For too long socialists have failed to provide a thorough analysis of 'the media'. The implications for socialist politics of the development of the enormous electronic communications industry, for example, have been sadly neglected . . . At worst socialists have ignored the whole question and viewed 'communications' as something which has undergone no substantial change since the 19th century.

The forums, which involved most shades of opinion on the left, as speakers and audience, were at that time seen simply as a means of filling a vast 'silence' on the left and as a means of opening up a discussion on these neglected questions – questions which we believed were vital. In these terms the series was moderately successful, attracting up to 150 people per session. The introductions and the discussions were taped and the bulk of the essays here were rewritten, using that raw material. Some additional essays were commissioned to fill in obvious gaps in the series, though unfortunately television is still under-represented. Most of the contributors are not academics but either political activists in and around the media and/or media practitioners of various sorts, with a commitment to socialism.

The finished collection of essays represents probably the first 'overview' of the various strategies being offered by the socialist and feminist movements, for a genuine opposition to and eventual transformation of the mass media. For that reason, and because of the failure of these various strategies to engage each other in a fruitful debate, there is a certain degree of disparity and even contradiction between some of the contributions. This is only to be expected at this relatively early stage in the process of left cultural practice and theorisation. It is to be hoped that the openness and precision with which these ideas are here presented can in some way help to bring together practitioners and theorists from the various fields and approaches for some eventual mutual exchange and synthesis in a richer, more effective practice.

It is perhaps appropriate that the first contribution in this collection is by Raymond Williams. He has been Britain's most radical, consistent and prolific analyst of culture and the media in the last twenty years. During a period until recently dominated by all sorts of deterministic economisms, he virtually alone in Britain has held out for the autonomous determinacy and efficacy of culture and 'cultural struggle'. It is significant that in his later writing, particularly his article on 'Base and Superstructure'[1] and his latest book,[2] he has shifted significantly to the left, towards a much more rigorous relationship with Marxism. Certainly one can say that any advances within the field of cultural theory and practice will have to build on and critically come to terms with Williams' substantial work.

Several beginnings of critiques of Williams from the left have been offered recently – the most important being the debate between Terry Eagleton and Anthony Barnett in *New Left Review*.[3] Barnett makes by far the most useful stab at Williams' weaknesses, whilst at the same time dealing sharply with Eagleton's sectarian, vituperative excesses (which, incidentally, fail in any case to deal at all with Williams' substantial work on the mass media, with which we are primarily concerned). He challenges Eagleton's hasty analysis of Williams as a 'national populist' and goes on to situate him within a much more fertile 'problematic'. For Barnett, Williams' principal weakness is his 'culturalism' – not, as Barnett admits, a misconception common on the left. By this he means:

a strategic vision of socialist politics in its way parallel to that of economism. Where economist strategies for socialism rely upon the spontaneous momentum of industrial struggles to accomplish the overthrow of capital, Williams' early books contain a culturalist argument which is logically similar. He suggests that revolutionary change will be accomplished by the spontaneous intensification of cultural exchange, the deepening of free communication and the liberation of creative expression . . . For culturalism, like economism, is essentially a failure to comprehend that only a mass revolutionary abolition of the apparatus of bourgeois rule can inaugurate the transition to socialism – something neither wage militancy nor cultural innovation alone can ever achieve.[4]

It has become evident to myself and others since this collection was first mooted, in particular whilst involved in the discussions about and the production process of *Wedge* magazine, that it is precisely on the relation between cultural work – with its 'relative autonomy' – in and against the mass media, and a broader revolutionary political practice, that the principal work has still to be done. A debate about Williams' work very effectively situates the main problems confronting us.

But Barnett is not totally negative in his assessment of Williams' contribution:

I have argued that in this political account of society and history, Williams is idealist in the role he assigns to culture . . . But there is another contrasting side to his approach which is materialist. For in part precisely in order to endow culture with the causal weight necessary for it to finally determine change, Williams – to a unique extent – has stressed and studied the material history of cultural forms . . . while he has been idealist in the roles which he assigns to culture *within society*, he has at the same time been materialist in his treatment of practices *within culture* . . . he has always been unshakably solid when he has examined actual forms and types of communication, from vocabulary and dialects to newspaper formats and the architecture of the stage.[5]

It is in this latter area that the left has been weak – substituting 'conspiracy' theories of breath-taking simplicity for any detailed

research on the ways the media actually work. Williams' work could
be indispensable in preparing further theoretical elaboration of the
complex processes which constitute the media.

To return to the specific contribution that Williams has made to
this volume, preliminary critiques of this have already seen the light
of day. David Glyn[6] took issue with Williams' approach to the mass
media 'through an examination of their institutions' – precisely the
kind of approach that Barnett found most useful, even in its
incompleteness. The kernel of Glyn's critique is the following:

> In failing to recognise that shifts and changes in the ideological role
> of the mass media reflect changes in the balance of class forces –
> and eventually fundamental challenges to the institutions the
> bourgeoisie uses in order to rule – Williams moves closer to those
> who advocate a conspiracy theory of the media than he realises.
> Conspiracy theories and Williams' position both rest in a view of
> history which excludes the working class as an active agent at
> virtually any level.[7]

Certainly the only role/influence that Williams seems to ascribe to the
working class in this contribution is as almost passive, fragmented
'consumers' or alternatively (and this is the core of much of his work)
the unified repository or bearer of some unspecified working-class
'values' or 'culture'. The class struggle is intimated merely as a distant
back-drop, rather than as an active (but largely unconscious)
determinant of the shape of the media institutions. When Claire
Johnston refers to 'left-Leavisism' in her essay in this volume, she is
undoubtedly referring to positions of this type.

This criticism can be related very closely to those of Barnett in
terms of positing an autonomous cultural terrain with its own
internal dynamic. Williams' importance lies in the fact that he 'bent
the stick' in this (idealist) direction at a time when Marxist and
socialist thought was dominated by an equally dangerous error –
economistic materialism, which chained the cultural and 'ideological' to the economic base, as mere 'reflection'. It is now vital (and
possible) to re-integrate cultural and ideological struggle into a
thorough-going historical materialist practice, in a way which
recognises both its specific limitations and its potential for taking
forward the class struggle as a whole.

The possibility of this re-integration has been made actual partly by the influence of the work of semiology, which purports to be a materialist study of the production of meanings and signs. The dissemination of these ideas in Britain is at an early stage, with much of the work in French by people like Lacan, Kristeva and Barthes still untranslated. But their impact has already been felt, particularly in the realm of film theory and practice. It is significant that the three contributors to this volume who have made most use of the work of structural linguistics, semiology and psychoanalytic theory in their essays are all women – Gillian Skirrow, Claire Johnston and Mandy Merck. For it was in the area of an understanding of and struggle against women's oppression that the lacunae of traditional Marxism were most glaringly apparent. To quote Mandy Merck in this volume:

> The ensuing rehabilitation of psychoanalysis . . . can be seen as the result of this dual imperative: the desire to extend a materialist analysis into areas unworked by Marx and Engels, and a rejection of the 'conscious' as the sole area of sexual identity and operation. But feminist investigation was not its only point of entry into Marxist theory. The feminist problematic coincided with, and fed into, a new project of Marxist epistemology . . . This was the rejection of the humanist notion of the alienated subject, proposed as an integral being somehow external to or pre-existing the relations of production.

It is impossible here to give an adequate summary of these various theories – the three contributors mentioned attempt such an introduction with a fair degree of success, given its often inaccessible terminology. In particular the psychoanalytic dimension is extremely complex and one of which the present writer is neither confident nor totally convinced. Nevertheless there are certain evident implications for cultural and political work in and around the media.

Semiology, as a body of theory, enables us to radically re-form our view of the media, to view television, the language of the mass press or film, as active systems of signification which contribute their own meanings to any 'message', as does the recipient. The 'receiver' of any 'message' is never passive – here we see the false analogy with the radio-receiver – but is an active *producer* of meanings. It is precisely one of the ideological functions of the bourgeios media to obscure this – the relations of consumption of the cinema, for example, attempt to reduce the process of *creation* of meanings on the part of the audience to an absolute minimum. It is interesting that we can see very strong parallels between this radical view of the process of 'communication' and Brecht's theories of the theatre, which always stressed the necessity for the involvement and creativity of the audience – its 'freedom' to choose, to select, to decide and ultimately, through criticism, to change any given production.

We have here then a much more complex and difficult model of the media: from the originator (himself/herself/themselves – not discrete, undivided 'subjects') through a whole series of codes embodied in signs which presuppose a particular reading, to the recipient, who also produces different meanings according to the relations of consumption and her/his relation to the message. Such a view of the media, not as passive communication but as an active, creative process involving the production of meanings which intimately relates transmitter, mode of transmission and 'consumer' in a unified complex process, precludes any conception of media 'distortion'. Distortion in the media, always implicitly linked to one 'conspiracy theory' or another, presupposes some 'pure' message which ought to pass unsullied through the media from start to finish, if it were not for the interference of active, reactionary agents or abstract ideology. It also presupposes an 'essential' reality which is being 'misrepresented' in some way or another. It is this view which Mandy Merck spends some time undermining in relation to orthodox views of 'sexism in the media'.

We can see then that a view of the signification process of the media as a whole, in its specific economic, political and social location in which meanings have constantly to recreate themselves and be created, is much more useful for understanding the role of the media in the production of ideology. It must supersede the view inherited from an outdated epistemology in which the receiver and the means of transmission are passive or 'mute'.

The second main conclusion we can draw from these theories involves the forms of opposition and resistance which are necessary within and against the bourgeois media. This is obviously an area central to the concerns of this volume. Bourgeois ideology is located not simply in the 'content' of a television programme or film in the orthodox sense – changing plots, narrative or characterisation is inadequate as a strategy. Bourgeois ideology resides precisely in the way that a particular 'reality' is constructed in the media – in the signs or 'chains of signification' which go to make up the 'language' of television or film or the theatre. Things like camera angles, conventions of representation, lighting, editing, 'pace' – all techniques which are seen as 'natural' – act as codes of meaning to construct a particular (bourgeois) reality. Once this is grasped – and Mandy Merck and Claire Johnston explain in greater detail how these processes work – then we can see that a central part of any strategy of 'oppositional' cinema or theatre or music (if we can 'decode' bourgeois conventions within music to begin with, in order to recognise them) must lie in what has been called 'the subversion of codes', the deconstruction of the codes in which a bourgeois worldview, via the media, is located.

Such a view widens the area of resistance in the media – it is no longer simply limited to the expropriation of the media, or the imposition of a 'political line' on a cultural product, in terms of plot. These possibilities have been particularly exploited, with mixed success, in the area of film.

However, it would not be fair to pass on without considering some of the weaknesses or dangers represented by the exponents of this current. The principal danger, which is ever-present, is that of descent (ascent?) into a new idealist formalism which deals exclusively with the 'signs' in language or the media, the ways they are articulated or perceived, and the mode of transmission – at the expense of what is being signified (that is, the material world and our interaction with it, which gave rise to the need for language in the first place).

Related to this are two other dangers. The first is outlined by David Glyn in his essay, which is in effect a critical reply to Claire Johnston. He criticises what he sees as an attempt to create a new, autonomous haven of 'ideological struggle' totally cut off from the class struggle as a whole or the determining political/economic social formation. Exponents of semiology have argued for the necessity to recognise 'moments' of theoretical and ideological resistance, but this easily slips over into an absolution from dirtying one's hands on the practical, political terrain. Particularly in the case of film it results in a failure to confront the very real economic and political situation in the film industry in Britain with anything resembling a strategy.

This leads on to the third weakness or danger in the semiological approach – particularly those variants of it underpinned heavily by Lacanian psychoanalysis. The semiological/structural approach to language has been unable to draw any conclusions about how one could change the present tactical/strategic goals of political action. Certainly the only field in which such theories appear to have prompted practical experimentation is women's cinema, in the work of Laura Mulvey and Peter Wollen in particular.[8] However, extreme conclusions from the work of Lacan could go beyond this, to a decisive repudiation of all forms of orthodox political activity, particularly for women. If sexist ideology, patriarchy, is embedded in language *per se*, then one pessimistic conclusion that can be reached is that political language and activities involving language are themselves ideological, and therefore problematic. This is a 'logical conclusion' which has not been adequately dealt with.

*   *   *

The bulk of the rest of the book concerns itself with a totally different set of 'strategies' some of which, in different forms, have long been advanced by the revolutionary left. The essays by John Thackara, Geoffrey Sheridan and myself, Dave Bailey and Tariq Ali all address themselves to questions of mass political opposition to the present media, moves towards workers' control of the media and the future administration and organisation of those media in a post-capitalist society. The relations between these tactics and conceptions and the theoretical work involving semiology which we have just discussed are unclear. Indeed, this volume is probably the first in which these two strategies have confronted each other – dialogue, interchange and mutual criticism between these two currents is to date non-existent, though a vital theoretical and practical necessity.

However, we can immediately take note of the fact that in all these latter essays the writers (and this includes myself) operate with a totally transparent, passive view of the media as, in Mandy Merck's phrase 'envelopes around true or false messages'. In particular Dave Bailey talks about 'taking over' or 'throwing open' the media in a way which really does beg all the questions about representation and ideology in the media which the semiologists have spent some time in elaborating. The media cannot be viewed just as abstract technical resources outside ideology.

The emphasis on the vitally necessary but long-term expropriation of the media as part of the process of revolution has led to a total neglect of those forms of 'cultural opposition' which can and must be developed now both within and without the media as precursors of a future revolutionary culture. In the last essay in the book I attempt to draw out the origins of such a neglect in the positions of Trotsky and Lenin, and its dangers. Such a 'silence', however, ultimately rests on an inadequate theorisation of the role of cultural struggle within the social totality and the revolutionary process as a whole. Vulgar base–superstructure models of society, which have bedevilled Marxism's attempts to comprehend the stability and hegemony of capitalism in the twentieth century, underlie such a lack of theorisation.

However, the most positive feature of these latter essays is their prolonged discussion of the whole vexed question of the relation of the mass media, their control and forms of democracy in future socialist societies. In this respect it is the negative experiences of the Soviet Union and the other workers' states and their dreadful example in the eyes of the working class of the advanced bourgeois democracies which have done most to discredit the ideas of socialists and communists.

Tariq Ali's essay offers the most extensive discussion of this problem, though most of the others touch on it in a very direct way. However, Tariq's contribution itself raises a whole series of questions which are worth further consideration.

In discussing the Cuban revolution he talks about it being the first 'television revolution' and claims that Fidel Castro used television very 'creatively.' But the forms of television propaganda which Fidel adopted were very orthodox, authoritarian and one-dimensional. The set-piece programmes were four-hour transmissions of Fidel's speeches – surely any socialist must reject such an authoritarian and monopolistic use of the media. It is interesting to note that one feature of the relations of consumption of television in Cuba did work against the bourgeois model of how television operates. Because there were relatively few sets, *collective* viewing of television was the norm in Cuba – as, for example, it is very much the norm in Italy, even today, in the bars and cafes. Such a situation cuts across the isolation, fragmentation and atomisation of viewers in the nuclear family. It also facilitates collective responses to programmes, in the form of discussions afterwards.

It seems to me that this points in some ways towards the relations of consumption of television that we would want to encourage in a socialist society. Television viewing would be a much more *collective* activity, involving groups of people with much larger screens in public places. Within the programming there would have to be forms of 'space' in which the audience could discuss and interact – through radio, telephone or possibly other television link-ups – as feed-back would have to be maximised.

Another point in Tariq's essay worthy of comment concerns Portugal and the famous '*Republica* affair'. His discussion of this event shows us clearly the complexity and difficulty involved in assessing such concrete situations. A look back to Dave Bailey's essay will show a totally different evaluation of the *Republica* experience. Dave Bailey recognises that the primary motive for occupying *Republica* was to safeguard jobs – the Socialist Party line in Lisbon was so unpopular that sales of the paper had plummeted and the paper was in danger of closing. Tariq argues that this occupation and take-over was a mistake and that the revolutionary workers should have simply taken over a page or two of the paper to expound their views. He tends to ignore the fact that the Socialist Party had many organs of propaganda besides *Republica*. In any case, there is no evidence that such a half-hearted transformation of the paper would have made it more popular and thus saved their jobs – a very pressing, material concern. However, what undoubtedly they should have done – and herein lies their omission – was to give one or two pages *back* to the Socialist Party for their propaganda. Undoubtedly the Socialist Party would have refused them, but such a move would have undermined the right-wing capital which the Socialist Party made of the affair.

The other point I wish briefly to discuss, related to Tariq's useful sketch or plan of how the media would operate in a post-capitalist state, is the question of whether the government or the state would have its own organ as well as the various parties and groupings. The problem here resides in the fact that a government organ would undoubtedly express the views of the ruling party, in addition to that party's own paper or television or radio station. In other words the party in power would have a decidedly unfair advantage, in terms of propaganda resources, over all other groupings. Such a discrepancy could well be one of the means by which the governing or majority party maintained its position. Such a situation, backed up by the undoubtedly superior resources of the state, compared with party or individual/group resources, would drive a carriage and pair through any formal equality and opportunity in the field of media.

*   *   *

Not all the contributions in the book fall squarely within the orbit of one or other of the two 'strategies' or approaches outlined earlier. Nevertheless, the contributions by Leon Rosselson and Ian Hoare and Gary Herman cover important new ground in a real sense. Music and popular music in particular, has remained almost totally untheorised or undiscussed by Marxists, with the exception of Adorno's somewhat technical, inaccessible texts. This is so despite the fact that many sections of the world revolutionary movement have created and extensively employed the powerful weapon of song as an integral part of its political culture – the American movement (in the shape of the Industrial Workers of the World – the 'Wobblies'), the French, Italian and Spanish workers' movements are obvious examples. The reasons for that theoretical neglect are beyond the scope of this present contribution, but undoubtedly such a silence rests on the problem that music presents for a traditional Marxist cultural analysis. This is based on the dichotomy between 'form' and 'content', as elaborated, for example, in the influential work of Ernst Fischer.[9] Such a dichotomy implicitly informs the essay by Leon Rosselson. Non-vocal music is impossible to analyse in this way, however, as form and content collapse into each other. Instead of reading this exception as a symptom of the unsuitability and ultimate unviability of such a model, Marxism has instead turned its back on the problem while maintaining the theoretical division in other fields.

With the growth of commercial music since the early 1950s, and its influence and popularity amongst wide sections of youth, this weakness in traditional Marxist theory has made itself felt more and more deeply. It was in part because of the pressing practical need to come to grips with this inadequacy that the organisation Music for Socialism was set up late in 1976. It consisted of musicians, music writers and other activists in the field, with a positive commitment to socialism, who wished to interact, share ideas, discuss theory and evolve new forms of musical practice which could broadly be called 'political'. Leon Rosselson's clearly-articulated position, as outlined in his essay, became one of the clear poles of the wide-ranging debate which necessarily racked Music for Socialism in the first year of its existence. Indeed its clarity and its evolution from within a carefully-circumscribed practice was its main strength, amidst the 'booming, buzzing confusion' which seemed to characterise much of the discussion within Music for Socialism. Only the Maoist group,

People's Liberation Music led by Cornelius Cardew – once one of Britain's leading avant-garde composers – advanced anything like as clear a position. For them music must be brimming with 'revolutionary content' (that is, the lyrics must be *about* revolution) otherwise it will slip inexorably into the camp of bourgeois reaction and counter-revolution. The worst epithet which could be ascribed to any musician by People's Liberation Music is 'formalist' – which rather begs the question that confronts Marxism in any consideration of music, as remarked on earlier.

Ian Hoare (a founder member of Music for Socialism) and Gary Herman have attempted to respond to these problems, particularly those put forward by Leon Rosselson, who has undoubtedly earned a valued and respected place for himself and his music on the left in Britain. In particular they are able to take a dialectical and creative view of the modern waves of music, particularly 'punk' music and its social co-ordinates, which Rosselson is so keen to dismiss. We hope the debate opened here will engender further discussion of these issues, both inside and outside the ranks of song-writers and musicians.

The theatre too has been sadly undertheorised, though it does have its influential revolutionary precursors in the shape of Meyerhold, Piscator and Brecht in the 1920s and 1930s. But a whole layer of committed, left-wing theatre groups has grown up in Britain in the last ten years as a response to the pressing needs of the class struggle, which knows little of these theorists and activists. Only some half-digested ideas of Brecht have permeated the frenetic, highly-charged and by necessity improvised world of the British 'agitprop' or 'fringe' milieu. In this field of cultural activity, as in no other, the exigencies of dire necessity and the politics of the situation into which these productions were inserted have played a crucial part in the political and artistic formation of the practitioners. Only recently, in the wake of the two-year downturn in the class struggle from 1974 to 1977 and the cutbacks in state funding in the arts (and in particular theatre groups), have certain sections of socialist and fringe theatre begun to recognise the need to step back, take stock and develop some sort of theoretical overview of their activity. Some preliminary stabs in this direction have appeared in the *New Edinburgh Review*[10] and *Wedge*,[11] which in particular attempts some analysis of the relations between state funding and the dramatic style and politics of the socialist theatre.

Chris Rawlence offers us the raw material of the experience of one of the oldest and best-established of the socialist theatre groups, Red Ladder. It too was forced to develop strategies purely 'internally' in the face of changing political circumstances in an empirical and piecemeal manner. Perhaps this clear exposition of the problems involved in left theatrical production, by one of its practitioners, can help stimulate a debate which can begin to transcend the present unparalleled crisis in British left theatre.

*　　*　　*

Lastly, from what has gone before we can sum up the areas of theoretical and practical work in the field of culture and the media which it will be necessary to develop and integrate if the politically vital work described is to go forward.

1. An analysis of the economic foundations of particular media and the specific productive labour processes which constitute the forms of cultural practice.

2. An analysis of the limitations which the above present to any media-form and the specific ways that such processes help 'naturally' articulate particular meanings.

3. An understanding of the process of signification within the media-process itself; the way the conventions of the particular media constitute 'sign-systems' which create new meanings.

4. Taking the complexities of points 1–3 into account, the elaboration of a *political strategy* which can begin to tackle the media as a whole, from minor forms of resistance, including the oppositional 'subversion of codes', to total expropriation. Such a strategy would of necessity have to articulate a relationship between cultural and ideological struggle and the political task of the seizure of state power.

5. A theory of democratic control and administration of the media and cultural practice in a post-capitalist society.

It is hoped that these essays can begin to fill in some of the gaps and preliminary stages towards the elaboration of such a genuinely revolutionary cultural theory and practice.

Chapter 1

The Growth and Role of the Mass Media[1]

Raymond Williams

We can start with the common view of the media on the left, which is that they are owned by the capitalist class to indoctrinate popular and working-class opinion. This is so often, in effect, true that for many purposes it is not necessary to look further. But once you apply your mind to the whole range of problems of these very different media in this kind of society, you find that you have to make the definitions at almost every point a good deal more precise.

For example, if you compare the organisation of the media as institutions in a capitalist society like Britain, in one like the United States, in one like France or West Germany, you immediately find significant differences. One difference is that in this country the press is very much more centralised. A national press is predominant in ways that it is not in France or West Germany or the United States. This immediately alters the whole status of the press as an institution.

Another point is that in this country, although there is now – after the pressure campaign of the 1950s – a commercial television network which resembles that of the United States in its majority services, we have had since the 1920s in Britain a very particular kind of organisation of broadcasting: the public corporation. This is still the majority service and the predominant one in sound. To define this in simple terms in relation to a capitalist economic system is obviously not easy. So the simple proposition that these are capitalist organisations already has to be qualified.

Returning to the point about the national press – a very specific feature of British capitalism – I think that nobody yet has found an adequate historical explanation for its dominance. It obviously has something to do with the earliness of the British Industrial Revolution and the development, at a time when the press itself was developing, of a railway network in a comparatively compact country. This enabled the national press to over-ride the provincial press and the local press in ways that were never possible in the United States and that were, on the whole, not attempted in France and Germany. But the predominance of the national press in this country affects the content and structure of the press in very specific ways, and there are quite observable political differences between the Fleet Street papers and the network of local and provincial newspapers. So that is a variation of structures.

The public corporation – this perhaps needs more careful analysis than anything in the whole media range, because of a familiar liberal tenet (which has some interesting evidence to support it) that the institution of an independent public corporation was a way of taking this most powerful medium out of the market and at the same time out of crude political control. Now again, if you compare an organisation like the BBC with the American networks or with state broadcasting systems in France, Italy, West Germany, you find a significant difference in the existence of that public corporation. At the same time, and this involves a quite complicated theoretical argument, it is impossible to live in this society, watching the behaviour of that public corporation, and accept the proposition of independence in the terms in which it is offered – an independence at a certain level from competing political parties. But is it really an independence from the state?

The fact is that there is something very specific about British culture which allows a different kind of organisation. We have an unusually compact ruling class with very deeply shared cultural assumptions and habits, which allows much of the effective state life of this country, things which would in other countries be the province of the state and of official agencies, to be delegated to public appointed authorities which have a certain measure of autonomy. If you look into the real relation of those corporations to the state, then you find of course that they are subject in financial policy finally to the state, that the heads of the organisations are appointed, a characteristic of this method, but are then given the kind of term of service which takes them beyond the patronage of any particular party government. Thus, if we look into the structure of the governors of the BBC, the governors of the IBA, comparable bodies like the Arts Council and so on, we see a very specific feature of British life.

Unless one analyses it carefully the slogan which we use is rebutted by what is actually no more substantial a slogan – that Britain has solved the problem, has moved between the twin dangers of the state control of the broadcasting service (which in France in the 1960s, for example, was complete) and the purely market service which is characteristic of the greater part of American television. We have to understand the specifics of this peculiar British structure of the autonomous, yet always essentially state-linked, organisation. That it is state-linked rather than state-directed is a crucial distinction.

The next point is that there is a very complex relationship between two factors which can be seen throughout the development of modern communications systems, and this leads us to have to make a much more precise diagnosis than the simple one of indoctrination.

Let me go back for a moment to the history of the press in this country. The press was almost entirely a creation of the bourgeoisie, mainly in the 18th century, against the remnants of a feudal and post-feudal state. The newspapers in the 18th century won their commercial independence and in the course of it a very important area of freedom of the press, including, for example, the right to report parliamentary debates, a battle which lasted a generation. Because the newspapers were linked to a precise commercial function they existed as combined news and advertising sheets – the advertising then, of course, being primarily classified advertising appropriate to that stage of the economy. But the battle against state control and state censorship has remained a permanent memory in the press as an institution and more widely in the whole society. This is why it is so difficult to talk about alternatives to the present system. That battle, which was real and which was fought over a hundred years, was against a very deliberate state attempt to prevent the emergence of the independent newspaper at all. It was not until the 1850s that the taxes on knowledge, the stamp duties on the press, were finally removed when the bourgeois class had finally reached ascendency in British society. So that fight is real and we must never forget it.

At the same time, that was still a very small press serving local communities or, where it was national, dispensing information from London to the provinces in what ultimately was a two-way process. In the early 19th century something very interesting happened – the emergence of an independent, radical press which preceded the availability of the vote. If you look at that early 19th century press, the *Political Register*, the *Black Dwarf* and all the others, or if you look at the very important institution of the Sunday paper, which preceded the daily paper by a long way in terms of popularity, you will find that this was the first popular press and that in its early stages it was essentially independent.

You must of course distinguish between the radical and the Sunday press, a matter which would take a long time. But just briefly: the radical press was tied to political campaigns, mainly then for the vote but also on direct economic issues; the Sunday press carried on elements of perhaps an older popular culture but certainly the new urban popular culture. It included a lot of reports of crime, a lot of reports of scandal – indeed, the Sunday newspaper as a distinct phenomenon is quite traceable from the 1820s to the present day – but it had a popular readership, often a collective readership when buying was beyond the finances of individuals. And even in those Sunday papers stories of crime and scandal were linked to radical politics because the audience was of that kind.

There is a popular myth which you can still find in quite standard histories that the popular press only occurred in Britain at the end of the century, in the so-called Northcliffe revolution, when people, having been taught to read by the board schools set up under the Education Act of 1870, had these cheap newspapers provided for them. This is totally untrue. At any time in the 19th century there were more than enough people who could read to sustain the modern circulation of the *Daily Mirror*. It was never a case of waiting for literacy, and the error of that history is that it is merely tracing the development of *daily* newspapers. But what happened in the early 19th century was the emergence first of the radical, campaigning newspaper and second of this very specific kind of Sunday newspaper with a mix of interest.

There was, then, a specific historical divergence. I have analysed this in *The Long Revolution*[2] and in 'Radical and/or Respectable',[3] but briefly there are two phases. The campaigning, radical press was attacked, legally and politically, on a scale amounting to open repression. But this alone would not have defeated it. From the 1830s on, with new and expensive printing technology, and with the new railway distributive system, the level of necessary capitalisation rose very sharply, and competition between the commercial press and the radical press entered a quite different phase. At the same time a popular readership was there and over the next forty years its interests and expectations were in effect incorporated into the commercial press, leaving the independent radical press – attacked first by political repression, then weakened by the basic changes in the economics of production – increasingly isolated. It then constituted a political popular press, without capitalist resources, facing a commercial version of the popular press, which was to become a major sector of capitalist development. The really crucial economic changes did not come through until the last quarter of the century: in the Sunday papers followed by new evening papers followed eventually by new daily papers.

Following general developments in the economy, the process of cultural incorporation was succeeded by moves towards corporate and quasi-monopoly ownership and control. Papers which had been independent until the 1880s – most newspapers were typically owned by one printing family or printing house – were incorporated in the first versions of the corporate press-houses that we have today. In the 1880s and 1890s what happened was firstly the emergence of corporate organisations of great bodies of newspapers and magazines owned by a single owner or firm; secondly, and this is crucial, the incorporation of advertising money of a new kind as the basis of a cheap paper. It is a fact of 19th century history that however popular the papers were, and however much advertising there was on the streets, there was hardly anything in the press except classified advertising. Northcliffe's revolution was to bring display advertising into the economic organisation of the press and on that basis sell the paper well below cost. That has been the specific economics of the British press ever since.

As everybody knows, because the crises are recurrent, the British press has since that time never sold on its ordinary revenue from readers. It has essentially been dependent on large supplies of advertising revenue of a block kind, to the extent where it accounts for anything between 50 per cent and 70 per cent of revenue in the daily and Sunday press. Now this leads to a very important effect. In the last twenty years we have seen one national newspaper after another disappear in financial crises. One was sorry at the loss of some of them, at best indifferent at the loss of others. But it has a had a particular political effect – there is no national press that I know of which has as limited a political spectrum as ours. Basically, as you go leftwards you stop at the *Guardian* – at least for fully distributed newspapers. There is nothing to the left of that. This is very unusual, in even quite comparable capitalist societies.

Furthermore, those national papers which closed – the *News Chronicle*, the *Daily Herald*, the old radical Sunday newspaper *Reynolds News* – all had very large circulations by comparison with those of any other capitalist society. That is to say, they closed with their circulation typically between one million and two million. The largest circulation of any newspaper in France, a similar size country with a very similar kind of economic organisation, is today about 650,000. How is it that this closure of papers (including on the whole a much higher than average proportion of papers on the left) has happened within this very specific press structure? It is because the press economy since that reorganisation in the 1890s has been based not on how many papers you can sell – because on that criterion papers could survive in this country in the same way that they do in France on circulations much lower than the present level of viability – but on the availability of advertising money. And in this way, in a much more interesting way than simply the fact that the owners of the press are capitalists (which is self-evident), you have a tie between the press and the nature of this specific capitalist economy which directly affects the range of newspapers that are made available.

The possibility of starting new papers, the possibility of maintaining a full political range, are determined by this fact. Why did the *News Chronicle* die? Because it had a large proportion of elderly, and in advertising agents' terms class C, D and E, readers. In other words for an advertiser it was not an important medium whereas for people reading the newspaper it was still very important. This is happening and I would like to predict will continue to happen because at the moment not more than two or three of our national newspapers can be guaranteed a life beyond five years. Now this is not just a general feature of capitalism to be resolved into a slogan. It is a very specific feature of British capitalist society and a now very deeply embedded structure of the development of the press economy in Britain.

It is at this point that one has to introduce the other complication, which is the contradiction between the bourgeois market and what is a perfectly straightforward, discoverable intention of managing news and opinion. It is not indoctrination. Indoctrination involves a much more controlled, authoritarian set-up than this one. You can talk of indoctrination if you like in a school where you have a captive audience. You cannot seriously, I think, talk only of indoctrination where people can choose at least over a limited range and in which they can choose whether to take the thing or not at a quite basic level.

What you have is something more interesting and something which explains many of the local contradictions in which people working in the media and people observing it find themselves caught – because at a certain level, if you look at the economic interests and the political affiliations of the people who own the press, it is not surprising that the press puts the kind of political and social line it does. The effects of this are very deep. They select the issues, they select the ways of treating them, and there is for us a permanent and necessary task of defence and enlightenment against those procedures.

On the other hand, there is all the time another kind of pressure. For example, take the phenomenom of the *Daily Mirror*, which began as a simple picture paper, in a fairly typical ideology of the early 20th century, for women. Women would not want to read about politics – in any case they did not have the vote – but they would like to look at pictures, they would like to read some gossip, they would like the events of the day treated in a lively way. This was the ideology of first the *Sketch* and then the *Mirror*. Now take the transformation of the *Mirror*, which occurred in the 1940s. Transformation is perhaps a strong word, but in any case a substantial alteration. The *Daily Mirror* campaigned in a radical way, as it said, on behalf of the men in the army. It campaigned at a certain level against the old ruling class. That adjective 'old' is important, because it is still a way of identifying that radicalism – you campaign against the 'old' ruling class and not the current one. It had a distinct political shift which at a certain level does not correspond directly to the political affiliations or the economic interests of its owners.

Now take this problem across for a moment to the case of the content of BBC and ITV. It is the basis of some interesting comparisons between them. If the purpose were what we sometimes say it is in understandable anger at some blatant political management of the news – in other words, indoctrination – then there would be certain things which got done on ITV and BBC, which got reported in the press, which would never be there at all. You have only to go to a really managed news system – read a Spanish newspaper, for example (until about two years ago), or go to a good deal of the East European press – to see what a system which is really concerned with excluding other points of view, other kinds of fact, is really like. Here again, as you compare this system with those systems, a liberal proposition is waiting which says: 'Here, after all, the press is open to all points of view, it reports the facts as they are, it reports the argument as it runs, with contributions from all points of view'.

Actually something much more interesting is happening. At a certain level the ideological function, which in certain parts and on certain issues is very explicit and is often a quite identifiable part of the internal structure of an organisation, is contradicted by the requirements of a bourgeois market of an ordinary kind. These people, precisely because they are of the class that one identifies, are interested in making profit in a competitive market with their particular commodity as against others. What is true at that level of the capitalist market has been true between the major broadcasting corporations since there have been two competing for an audience. At this point something more interesting than indoctrination begins to occur. And this is the process which in the end you have to analyse as the attempt to incorporate – which, however, is always likely to fail if it is done in too crude a way, and which typically requires people from outside the old ruling class to do it.

This is the most interesting phenomenon of the last thirty years. Here is a brief example from the BBC/ITV competition of the late 1950s and early 1960s. People say now: 'What a breath of life ITV brought to television as against the stuffy old BBC. How they pushed forward the frontiers of television'. And at that level it is true. If you look at what the BBC was like before there was competition it is true, because the BBC was then in its old sound radio position, where the unity of the culture rather than any particular political intention was expressing itself in a particular set of relationships with listeners and viewers. These were always the relations of an educated class to – the usual word is – 'uneducated'. This word 'uneducated' (which lasted after eighty years of compulsory education – a very interesting commentary on the education system) was the word they used. Or the 'half-educated', which is an equally interesting concept. If you look at it, the distinctly identifiable upper-class culture (even when they were being entertaining, the tone was still there) was by-passed – by what?

Not by British popular culture – that is the trap that is prepared for one, in the official accounts of the developments of that organisation: that the old, stuffy, upper-class monopoly was swept away by a wave of popular, democratic sentiment, as the first Director-General said. No, but by American imports! The British working-class audience, faced by a choice between American imports and what the English upper class was offering it, fairly quickly made its preferences felt.

At this point there is great danger of taking what is a purely market phenomenon, with interesting implications for the state of mind of the society, as if it were a popular phenomenon; and the same thing is true about the *Mirror*. If you look at what the *Mirror* campaigned about after the war, it is very illuminating. I remember reading it then and reading it on through the elections of the 1950s. In the election of 1955, for example, I remember sitting in a polling station at 7 o'clock in the morning. There on the front page of the *Mirror* was a picture of Sir Anthony Eden at Eton, and I was sitting, to my embarrassment, with a working-class woman who was the Tory teller. She said: 'I don't think his lot will get in', although she was telling for his party! One of the complications of British life . . .

If you look at the situation, the resentment or the contempt or the sense that these are *other* people was very skilfully incorporated. The whole language of the *Mirror* through that evolution from the 1940s to the 1950s was a very skilful miming – it is miming – of colloquial English, to reassure people that these are not the all-too-familiar voices of the established culture but these are people like yourself. You knew you couldn't even say, as Richard Hoggart pointed out years ago, something like, 'It's going to rain', which is colloquial enough. You had to say, 'Take a mac, mate', because that sounded folksy. It established the sales, and these were skills which were highly rewarded. Let us not underestimate them: they took a long time to work out – at a certain level you had to persuade people that you were speaking for them and in their way against this identifiable old culture which was not theirs, although obviously as an institution, and on every decisive level of political choice and economic affiliation, the very organ doing it was part of the class which it was presumably rejecting. But precisely what it was rejecting was an *old* ruling class, and so it could not be identified with something as substantial as IPC, which is a *modern* ruling class institution.

This means that we must be very careful when we talk about indoctrination. On the one hand, what is happening is not as simple as that; and on the other hand, as it is perceived that it is not as simple as that, there is a very easy relapse into a position which I have seen a good many people get into, and which is a particularly dangerous one. Failing to understand the inwardness of the phenomenom – and it is a very deep one – people acquire a contempt (which is always possible in the political vanguard) for the majority of their fellow countrymen. They say: 'How can they be fooled by that? How can they choose to take in the propaganda, the selection of views and opinion which is so obviously that of another class?'

You can only understand this phenomenom – and it is a very complex one in the way it works out – if you put forward the notion of incorporation rather than indoctrination. That is to say, it is crucial for that kind of popular press – as it was for the incorporation of the genuinely independent popular press of the early 19th century – that the real interests of the majority of readers within existing society be spoken to. You had to include their interests – the crime was there, the scandal was there, because people wanted to read them. The sport was there as organised sport developed. Without these interests the old independent political papers of the first half of the century could not compete, although when it came to political opinion on its own, whenever it could be tested, they still held the majority of the class. But when it came to buying a paper, there were all these other competing interests.

The very fact of a politically campaigning paper, the independent paper, excluding the existing cultural affiliations of the majority of its potential readers, has this self-defeating effect. The commercial popular press, which is a very specific thing, is extremely careful to incorporate, and it learns a language for its political argument. It learns a language for its handling of news which at a very deep level involves the process of the self-identification of the reader with much that is apparently being spoken. This is done, if not in their name, then apparently from their position and with their kind of life-style and interests. And this is often very different from what they will hear if they talk to someone actually much closer to them in political interest and in real experience, who has become politically committed.

This has also happened in commercial advertising on an extreme scale with the careful miming of other people's feelings – for example, taking great care to get the actress to look like a housewife who cannot quite say 'biological' without being trained, if she's going to talk about a washing powder. This is the craft of people who understand that 'biological' might be a trick word and who therefore get the identification.

All of this is of course a trick, but understanding it is the theoretical correction to our simple received notions of indoctrination. Of course, that does occur in certain places at certain times, but it is the incorporation which I think is the true challenge to the left. If you think incorporation only happens to other people, then I just say you are lucky. Because every time I've ever done any analysis of this, I've found how many of my own responses are triggered. Take one that I'm a sucker for, just to conclude: I'm a Welsh rugby fan, so when somebody wearing a Welsh rugby jersey comes on with a pint of someone's beer and says 'Boyo' (of course he has to say 'Boyo', he doesn't say 'chaps') then I really have to work it out.

The point is that we are faced with very specific phenomena of late capitalist society which we are very often still describing in the terms of early capitalist society. In terms of their economic structure, the increasing movement towards corporate monopoly ownership, the exclusion of media which do not meet their economic criteria, the steady control (of which we should be increasingly reminded) of the so-called independent public corporations by the very fact of appointment from the state at their controlling levels – all these phenomena demand the most detailed investigation. My argument is that if we look at their historical evolution we can find the material for this analysis and so learn a new language for addressing ourselves to the problems of the media in our own times.

Chapter 2

Education and Television: Theory and Practice

Gillian Skirrow

Television and school are in many people's minds opposed: watching television is something you choose to do in your leisure time, whereas school is often associated, at best, with work and obligatory attendance. But these institutions together occupy a significant part of our time, which they fill with meanings, directing us into a particular way of making sense of the world. And the extent to which this 'sense' is exactly a common one seems to me more significant than the apparent differences between the institutions.

Objective Knowledge

Both education and television claim to report 'impartially' and to pass on 'objective knowledge'. Their ultimate goal is to describe and explain things as they are and were and can be predicted to be in the future, and their assumption is that the truth of knowledge depends on the neutrality of the theorist/observer in relation to the object studied. This is based on a further assumption: that the theorist/observer/subject of knowledge is a unified consciousness which can stand outside meaning and is clearly separated from the object which it is studying, and that objects in the real world can be known to us as 'they really are'.

This assumption has been seriously challenged by recent work in semiology, notably by Julia Kristeva, and in sociology by Barry Hindess and Paul Q. Hirst. Such work has stressed the importance of discourse for theory. What can we know of objects in the real world except through discourse, which necessitates the involvement of a subject? How can a subject be a unified consciousness if the unconscious participates in thought (as maintained by Jaques Lacan, following Freud) and how can a subject be outside meaning if the subject is herself/himself constructed by the same process in which she/he learns how to mean? A theory of knowledge which assumes subjects and objects from the start, rather than one which tries to account for their production, is incompatible with a philosophy which is concerned to change the world

The material conditions of existence of the institutions of education and television, however, dictate that they are not committed to changing things, particularly not themselves, and so their philosophy is one which maintains a belief in the importance of the subject/object distinction. It does not even embarrass them when two or more observers/theorists who claim to be neutral come to different conclusions about the 'objective facts'. The problem is resolved by calling such disagreements 'value judgements' or 'partialities' or 'points of view'; neutrality can then be restored by recourse to another assumption: that the expression of a plurality of partialities or viewpoints represents objective truth. The expression of this plurality in education is called 'academic freedom' and in the media 'free speech' or 'freedom of the press'. What does cause embarrassment for the institutions, however, is the questioning of their assumptions about given subjects and objects and the related assumption of a notion 'communication' which is somehow privileged, is outside the system of subjects and objects, and meaning. It is supposed to be a neutral milieu through which 'messages' are 'transmitted'. The idea that the expression of plurality may not amount to 'truth' or even 'freedom' is a very difficult one for the institutions to deal with. Anyone who proposes this idea will quickly find the limits of freedom within these institutions. The idea will usually be censored and often, in an interestingly catch-22 way, by an appeal to the need to keep 'communication' 'value-free'. A typical example of the perceived limits on academic freedom, which is also topical at the time of writing, comes from a supporter of anti-Marxist propagandist Julius Gould in a letter to the *Times Higher Education Supplement*:

since scholarship necessarily rests on the communication of ideas, it is essential that we should all safeguard the medium of that communication from the pollution of those who seek to distort it for tactical advantage.[1]

The Vice-Chancellor of the Open University, Sir Walter Perry, is also quite open about the limits on academic freedom at his university:

Total academic freedom on the part of all its staff could lead to use being made of the teaching programmes to indulge in polemic, enabling an individual member of staff to preach disaffection or even sedition to a very large audience.[2]

Sir Walter Perry goes on to say that 'polemic' (a more neutral word than 'pollution'?) is 'an understood part of the life of a university' so long as it takes place 'behind the doors of a classroom', but it seems to become more unacceptable and freedom more limited in proportion to the size of audience. Yet how can this be if communication is value-free and the audience made up of free subjects capable of making objective judgements about their experience?

Impartial Television

When the audience is the 'mass' of television viewers the ideas of objective knowledge and value-free communication have to be protected by law:

It shall be the duty of the Authority to satisfy themselves . . . that due impartiality is preserved on the part of the persons providing the programmes as respects matters of political or industrial controversy or relating to current public policy.[3]

An IBA document further defines 'current public policy':

Current public policy need not be about a matter which is obviously in the field of controversy. There are certain matters on which there is a broad consensus between the Parties or which, because they are temporarily dormant, do not at present cause controversy, but which could, once raised, affect public policy.[4]

The BBC is under similar restrictions. The necessity for impartiality, for balance, was seen carried to its logical, ludicrous conclusion in a BBC *Man Alive* programme on South Africa (on 12 December 1974) which suggested that there could be a neutral stand on exploitation and racism. The programme showed part of *Last Grave at Dimbaza*, a film which tried to give some idea of the poverty and oppression of blacks in South Africa, but the film had to be cut by nearly half so that it could be 'balanced' by a film specially provided by the South African government which showed black people driving around in cars in the apparently affluent and happy township of Soweto.

Outrageous as this piece of television was, at least it provided an opportunity for part of *Last Grave at Dimbaza* to be shown. Very often, controversial ideas such as those of this film never reach the screen, partly because of the technical and legal difficulties involved which would interfere with the smooth running of tight schedules, and partly because producers censor themselves, knowing what would be unacceptable. Quite apart from the existence of the Independent Broadcasting Authority Act, however, such ideas are rarely suggested because they are not thought to be what the majority of the audience wants. The audience, which has been produced by other social institutions, the family and school, can be predicted to be happy with a narrow range of received ideas packaged in two different styles as either information or entertainment. In output directed at the schools themselves there is rarely even a choice of style, education being seen by both schools and the broadcasting authorities as synonymous with 'value-free' information. In schools television, so predictable are the non-controversial topics that the schools want and the television companies are geared to producing that the ITV primary topic chart[5] for 1978–9 – which shows how often certain topics recur in all series – also shows the unchallenged and unchallenging narrowness of schools broadcasting. The major topics covered by programmes within series are grouped under the main headings animals, canals, castles, communities, farming, food/resources, health/road safety, jobs, other countries, seasons/weather, transport, and water/seaside. Health/road safety, animals, and water/seaside are the most covered topics.

According to the section on impartiality in the Independent Broadcasting Authority Act, the provision of such a narrow range could be contested. It would be interesting, for example, if a Marxist group made representations to the IBA that all the programmes on animals gave a one-sided picture of animals under capitalism. None of the programmes deals directly with the way capitalism exploits animals, turning them into ever more efficient production machines by force-feeding and battery-rearing. It could be maintained that the schools television output is politically partial, not to mention potentially controversial, on many matters of public policy. But such a suggestion would simply be laughed out of court by the IBA, whose business it is to interpret the Act; for capitalist or 'liberal' knowledge appears to be 'natural' rather than produced, 'the way things are' rather than ideas constructed by institutions within a particular political, economic and ideological system. 'Due impartiality' as practised by the institution of television has thus a very particular and limited meaning. It means that any programme content, any idea which might, if raised, cause controversy, must be accompanied by an opposing viewpoint within a series of programmes. It does not even mean that all viewpoints on the matter must be covered, and in practice it often means that a tory view will be opposed to a labour one, or an individual will be opposed to a representative of an institution. Television in general is therefore bound to be supportive of the *status quo*, and those in control of the institutions will readily admit to it:

> The structured orientation of the media in favour of . . . the forms of the democratic Parliamentary state . . . is perfectly patent and open . . . and already enshrined in the quite plain-spoken words of the Director-General himself: 'Yes, we are biased – biased in favour of Parliamentary democracy.'[6]

To say that television is biased in general in favour of parliamentary democracy, or that it is biased in its particular programmes, is to state the obvious; more significantly, however, it is to adopt exactly the same terms for argument as the institution itself. To attack the institution on the grounds of bias is to accept and to reinforce the idea on which the institution depends: that plurality of viewpoints equals truth. Director-Generals always reply to charges of bias that they have an equal number of complaints from the right and the left. In the end, it is said, the viewers will be able to judge from their own experience whether the institution is biased or not. There the argument about bias either stops or continues in circles.

What is never questioned is the position of the viewer, who is assumed to be the unified subject of knowledge standing outside the television message, outside the product of the television industry. And this is really where any critique of television's definition of itself as impartial communication should begin. For television is more than a product; it is a work, a work whose function it is to naturalise the social, the cultural, the product of class division, so that it seems to be 'the way things are'. Just as schools help to construct their pupils' identities by giving them, through language, a position in relation to knowledge, to teachers and to fellow students, so television, through its specific language, also puts and keeps its viewers in certain positions but in a way more difficult to see and so, perhaps, more difficult to reject. The 'medium' when 'properly used' is thought to be natural, neutral, value-free, innocent and so to guarantee the truthfulness of the 'message'. And yet what holds the attention in any story is the *telling* of it.

Language, 'communication', gives it recipient a place from which to view its 'message'. In this sense it can never be neutral, in this sense the notions of 'communication' and 'content-message' become impossible. In television things are always seen *from somewhere*, and the work of television is to give a perspective, a view of the world that is framed, harmonious and encourages the individual viewer to see herself/himself in a central position. Ideas of presenting facts impartially or objectively for the viewer to judge can only reinforce *the* view of television itself; they have the effect of giving the viewer a sense of being above and outside the actions displayed, and of having a god-like relation to them. How this specific language of television works to position the viewer can only be demonstrated through lengthy analysis of programmes,[7] but for present purposes a brief example of one positioning device will do. The example is from documentary, where a programme will often have someone either in vision or as a voice-over who will come to represent the point of view not only of the programme but of the viewer of the programme. He (it's usually a male) may be a television reporter or an 'authority', he speaks straight to camera and he will usually be given the last word.

This is the case at the end of a *World in Action* on 'The Nuts and Bolts of the Economy', transmitted in 1976. The programme was about investment, and the reporter summed up to camera:

It may be that industry will be reporting bigger profits. And you and I of course on the other hand, bound by the social contract, will see little if any greater profit in our weekly pay packets for our labours. It will be a strange experience to see bigger and bigger company profits reported whilst our pay packets don't benefit at all. But it shouldn't make us angry provided that the appropriate slice of those profits is ploughed back into new investments. If it isn't ploughed back, then we'll have the right to get very angry indeed. Goodnight.

A smart slap on the wrists for the managers of industry! The programme never, of course, questioned whether private ownership is the best way of running the economy but, more important than this, the viewer is given very little chance of coming to a different conclusion from that of the reporter, because of the *way* the story is told. For everything that has been seen has been seen from the reporter's apparent point of view, that of an objective observer who has summoned shop stewards and managers to appear before him, nicely composed for the camera/viewer but never addressing her/him directly to give their evidence for the programme. Having heard the evidence, which has been cut up into viewable chunks in 'interesting' juxtapositions which keep up the suspense and timed so that management and unions run to equal length, the reporter addresses the viewer directly and draws everything together into a unity, a coherence, making 'sense' of the evidence, *as seen* in the programme, for the viewer.

Towards a Different Television Practice

I have used the example of the reporter and his evidence in order to point out the difference between the conventional practice of documentary television and that of a series of programmes which tried to work from a different problematic. This was a schools series about mass communications in society. It was called *Viewpoint*, and it was made by Thames Television and transmitted in the autumn of 1975. Three of us wrote it: Alan Horrox, who was also the producer-director; Douglas Lowndes, Head of the Educational Advisory Service at the British Film Institute; and myself, as the education officer for the series, employed by Thames. For us the relation between theory and its object was less important than that between theory and practice. We would not concede that it was possible to be objective about the role of mass communications; instead we attempted to work out a new television practice which followed from an alignment with a working-class viewpoint. The questions we asked were not, 'How does television show reality?' but 'What is the reality of television's function in society?' The series was made up of ten programmes divided into three parts:

Part 1 set out the relationship between communications and society:
    Programme One, *Believe Me*, showed that communication is a way of building and maintaining our system of values and beliefs in society, and demonstrated that mass communications in this country mass-produce with great impact a narrow range of values and beliefs which form the received views of our society.
    Programme Two, *Communication is Control*, argued that throughout history communications technology has been consistently tied to the economic and political interests of power-holders in society.

Part 2 showed how all media messages, whether 'fact' or 'fiction', are shaped by the processes of production:
    Programme Three, *Money Talks*, illustrated from advertising material that all language, including that of visual image, is made up of symbols. This means that communication is always a construction, and never simply a reflection of the 'facts'.
    Programme Four, *News Story*, showed that news gathering and production is based on a set of supposed news values, which predetermines what *is* news.
    Programme Five, *Love Story*, showed how fiction and drama tend to reinforce stereotypes – for example, the traditional relationship of weak women and strong men – and how those stereotypes are related to the structure of society.
    Programme Six, *The Real Thing*, illustrated from documentary material the many choices that have to be made at every stage of production, and the way 'balance' works to support the *status quo*.
    Programme Seven, *Fun Factory*, showed how messages are shaped by being presented as belonging to certain categories – for example, information, education and entertainment.

Part 3 was about the structures of the media:
    Programme Eight, *Show Business*, looked at the industrial structure of the communications industry and showed how financial and

political pressure can influence the range and content of messages selected for mass production.

Programme Nine, *No Way*, described the limitations on access to the mass media by the mass of the people and pointed out that the media are centres of power over which there is no direct democratic control.

Programme Ten, *Action*, showed the range of small-scale media – 8 mm film, portable video, tape – slide, screen printing and litho printing – that can be used by schools or community groups to make their own messages.

Each programme had several elements, most of them recognisable from some familiar television or theatre form. There was the in-vision presenter (from documentary), songs and sketches (from revue and political theatre), animation (the radical potential of which had already been demonstrated by the *Monty Python* programmes); there was also film shot by radical film-makers and there were interviews with people who were normally viewers of television, which replaced both the more usual short 'vox pop' interviews with people in the street and the authority-figure interviews. These forms were used to contrast with and contradict clips from mass-media film and television which were also shown. So none of the elements was unfamiliar, and all used the accepted codes of scale of shot, narrative, and articulation of sound and image, but the elements were used or combined in ways which slightly refocused the usual meanings. There was the problem that much of what is intelligible and visually pleasurable is so enmeshed with the generally-held assumptions which *Viewpoint* tried to question that sometimes the element of questioning did not come through.

For example, the first programme tried to show that the mass media mass-produce a limited number of beliefs and in doing so they block the production of other beliefs. This was illustrated by mass-media material which presented competitive individualism as a natural and taken-for-granted concept to the exclusion of beliefs in co-operation and group effort. Several pieces of empirical research on this programme suggested that students sometimes felt that the programme was 'for' competitive individualism. So our practice sometimes paid the price for remaining within the bounds of intelligibility – it sometimes reinforced the supposed 'reflections' of 'reality', failing to show them up as structuring work. For the most part, however, the formula worked. The presenter's position was particularly clear. He did still represent the view of the programme but this view was acknowledged to be a committed one. Just as first-person narration in a novel is more distancing than that in the third person, so we expected that it would be easier for the viewer to distance herself/himself from a committed statement of 'viewpoint' than from the god's-eye-view of the impartial presenter. Since Douglas Lowndes did not represent 'the viewer' for the programme but a proletarian class interest, discussion afterwards could only with difficulty be posed in the terms of a liberal 'there's-a-lot-to-be-said-on-both-sides' debate. We hope also that Douglas's mode of address – straight-to-camera statements of belief – may have led students to look with new eyes at other presenters who are given the privilege of talking direct to camera – newsreaders, reporters, politicians and so on.

Other elements in the programme were similarly committed – they were not used in the conventional sense of evidence. From the first seconds of each programme, when a fist broke through a television screen in the opening titles, the purpose was to shatter the vision of representation, to give some idea of the work going on beneath it. This meant, of course, a break with ITV documentary house-style and it is significant that this was one of the most disturbing aspects of the series for the IBA, as is clear from an IBA report by the programme staff to the lay-members – the governing body – of the IBA:[8]

> The partisanship of the series lies not so much in the proposition [that most mass-media messages reflect the values of capitalist enterprise] as in the attitude of the presenter to capitalism and to privately owned media, which is consistently hostile; for instance, the extent to which capitalism facilitates freedom of expression within a pluralistic culture is not examined. *Above all the partisanship is expressed by the tone and the style of the programmes.* [Emphasis added.]

After discussing the report, which recommended that repeats of all the *Viewpoint* programmes should be allowed subject to some revisions, the lay-members demonstrated the extent to which capitalism facilitates freedom of expression by banning the retransmission of the series.

Theorising Television Practice

The importance of theorising the practice of television is not simply that television takes up a great deal of people's time – so does sleep – but because it occupies its viewers' time with meanings. As with other ideological institutions its function is to position people by the way it talks to them, or in the particular case of television to maintain positions already created by the operation of language in the institutions of the family and school. At the very least we can say that television maintains the intelligibility of social relations, an intelligibility which tends to serve the interests of one class, for part of the system of intelligibility is the concept of the 'free' wage-worker. The economic system of production of surplus value and its appropriation by capital needs subjects who feel themselves to be free. And since the system presents itself to the individual through television in such a way as to make the individual feel that she/he is above and outside the system and has a free and independent view of it, this makes the work of television important: the materiality of the institution of television is in its positioning of people in relation to discourse.

The work of television is less apparent than that of narrative film or the obviously constructed images of advertising posters. Television's images seem to be immediate and direct, natural, real, not man-made, and not in need of explanation. Perhaps one reason why there has been little theoretical work on the nature of television is that television itself works hard to achieve invisibility and often succeeds. *Viewpoint*, whose task was made all the more difficult by the lack of theory, forced the beginning of theoretical study as much by its ill fate and its effects on its own institution as by its presentations. The series was also a challenge to the schools who used it, since there is very rarely a 'media studies' slot in the curriculum. More often the series sat rather uncomfortably within existing subject areas such as English or social studies, which it confronted with a different kind of knowledge. It is indicative of the extent to which television is thought not to be in need of explanation that hardly anywhere throughout the education system does a subject called 'television studies' exist, but this lack of establishment as a separate area of study is not to be regretted considering the direction that 'film studies' sometimes takes both in higher education and in the schools, where film has become the object of a purely 'aesthetic' analysis – this in spite of the work of journals such as *Screen* and *Screen Education*, which have tried to place the study of film in its institutional and political contexts. It is important that the study of television should not be 'depoliticised' into something called 'television studies'.

There has been some theoretical work on television – particularly in the journals mentioned above, in the British Film Institute series of television monographs, and in the Working Papers of the Birmingham Centre for Contemporary Cultural Studies – but these writings are not well known among people working in television institutions, partly because of inaccessibility either of their style or of the distribution system. There has been a particularly significant study of television news by the Glasgow University Media Group:[9] although the study was concerned with content only and stopped short of an analysis of television itself, it had the merit of being read by many people in television. One of the greatest obstacles to theorising television practice is that there is little overlap between television practitioners and television theorists – they are two separate groups of people with quite different ways of talking about the practice of television; so much was obvious at the first Television Festival, held in Edinburgh in 1977. Part of the responsibility for the lack of communication must rest with the theorists, whose work is not accessible to practitioners, but part must also rest with television practitioners, who, like television consumers, usually do not see the need to theorise what they are doing – which is hardly surprising since they are part of the system which thinks of television as transmitting the essence of the real. The independent television union (the Association of Cinematograph, Television and Allied Technicians), for example, tries to keep watch on the programmes that the companies make and transmit, but its mechanism for doing this, the 'Bias in the Media' committee, is set up in the terms of the institution of television with the same definition of 'communication', the same taken-for-granted distinction between 'form' and 'content', and the same notion of 'bias'. This approach sees television as simply transmitting pre-existing messages, which suggests a conspiracy – the 'senders' of the messages are biased – so this approach retains the fundamental nature of the system it is attacking whereas what is needed is an approach which can break with the system as a whole.

Such an approach is one which recognises television as a *practice* which constructs systems of meaning, and which constructs them *for* somebody, a viewer, a subject, who is given a position, a view, in relation to those meanings. It also recognises that the people who write and make television programmes are not to be identified as the source to which something called 'bias' can be traced. The whole institution of television operates within certain limitations (for example, legal, financial and political) and it is these limitations imposed by its relation to the rest of society that gives it its point of view. This is, however, very different from saying that the institution of television is totally determined by the economy. To say, as I said earlier, that television maintains an intelligibility which tends to serve the interests of one class is not to reduce television practices to mere 'expressions' or 'reflections' of an 'economic base'; it means that television provides some of the conditions of existence of the structure of what Hindess and Hirst have called economic class-relations. The implications of a theory of total determination by the economy, whether in the last instance or otherwise, are that there could be no hope of change in television practice short of a revolution in economic relations, whereas the implications of a theory which sees television as an ideological/cultural form which secures the conditions of existence of a definite set of relations of production is that television practice, with its specific effects, must be taken seriously and has a real part to play in changing society.

What is needed is the theorising of a revolutionary practice for television, a practice perhaps which aims to unsettle the subject position of the viewer. It is not enough simply to take over ideas from Brecht's theatre or from contemporary film-makers (who are way ahead of television producers in theorising their practices), for though television's language may be a neighbouring one to that of film, and share some features with that of the theatre, it is not the same language. This theorising is only likely to have a practical outcome if those involved in practising in television are also involved in theorising it.

Perhaps the place to look for new developments is in educational television, either the schools departments of mass-media institutions or closed-circuit television within educational institutions. In these contexts groups of people have the opportunity to watch and discuss programmes together – some even have the facilities to record a programme and analyse it quite carefully. A programme's structurings become more apparent in such situations, and its work to produce meanings can be exposed. By discussing the ways in which these meanings are produced a group of viewers can question those meanings and work towards the production of new knowledge.

The critical viewing group also potentially provides a situation for which new kinds of intelligibility could be produced by a programme. Although this is at present far from being an accepted part of educational television practice, I think there is even now more room for discussion over what an educational programme should be like than there is, for example, over current affairs or even drama output.

John McGrath, in his 1976 MacTaggart Memorial Lecture, deplored the rigidity of television drama:

> Are we going to allow television drama, then, to carry on churning out *Son of Barlow*, and imitations of imitations of imitations? Are the new writers coming into television going to carry on believing naturalism *is* television? And that all you need to do is select your little corner of reality and turn it into a family drama with five sets? Are we going to encourage lazy, uncritical thinking, to step round theoretical discussion in true British fashion as if a dog had dropped it?

The answer to all these questions is 'probably', since in television drama, as John McGrath points out, 'the meaning of form is no longer discussed'; naturalism is 'what goes'. But it is a pity that John McGrath seems to see the possibilities of television only in terms of television drama. Theoretical discussion and space for radical practices are more likely to be found in a situation where the audience is not regarded as consumers whose only means of communication with the television institution is to switch their sets on or off.

So what is to be done? What are the implications of accepting that educational television provides one of the few spaces within which the question of the production of knowledge and meaning can be explored? Theoretical work on educational television needs to be done, and it needs to be done not to create an audience for itself but with the aim of helping television practitioners. Those of us who are teachers, students or viewers need to inform ourselves and make our contribution to the debate. Also writers and directors in television should note John McGrath's final remark in the MacTaggart Lecture that they 'need to acquire the habit of theoretical discussion before churning out another ten years of naturalism'. Theoretical work on its own will not, of course, be any use. New practices have to be tried and encouraged, and theorists would do well to turn their attention to television texts that do attempt to do something different instead of getting bogged down in descriptions of standard-output programmes. Those of us who have access to small-scale video equipment can also help practitioners by trying out ideas and constantly relating theory to practice. Another implication is that since the allocation of the fourth channel is being discussed at the moment, everyone interested in developing a radical television practice should press for an expansion of adequately financed educational broadcasting.

Chapter 3

Pop Music: Mobiliser or Opiate?

Leon Rosselson

It is generally agreed that song is the most powerful emotional force of all, capable of stirring people into violent action or dulling them into a state of stupefied numbness. 'La Carmagnole' is supposed to have played a crucial part in winning the French Revolution. The ferocious hymn-singing of the Hussites reportedly caused the Crusaders to flee in terror. Songs have given fight to the Kentucky miners in the 1930s and heart to the civil rights demonstrators in the 1960s. Songs have been proscribed as dangerous and kept from the ears of the common people by such exalted authorities as Queen Elizabeth I and the Controller of Radio One.

'Give me the making of a nation's songs', said somebody, or if he didn't he ought to have done, 'and I care not who makes its laws.'

One way or another, song is clearly a serious business, and if the raising of political consciousness, as the jargon has it, is a prime task for the left, song ought to be a powerful weapon.

But, of course, it is not. More than any of the other performing arts, the world of song is dominated by the money men on the one hand and the moral censors of the media on the other. The possibility of alternative voices making themselves heard is always small and at times, such as now, non-existent.

The illusion is that song is a freely available commodity. It belongs to everybody. Song is everywhere, blasting through the loudspeakers, filtering through the walls and the cracks in the ceiling, floating over the park, jingling around in your head even when you don't want it to. The reality is that song is the private property of business organisations, and by 'song' I mean not only individual songs but the whole song idiom; the idiom in which you might find your own voice has been appropriated by the market.

The industry that turns people into consumers and music into a product for leisure-time consumption is run on much the same lines as any other industry. Like any manufacturer a record company invests in a product and expects to see a return on that investment. The investment may be anything up to and beyond £50,000 to equip, groom, dress, package and promote a group or artist. Charisma, one of the few smaller companies to have carved out a share of the market for themselves in recent years, spent £100,000 on promoting Peter Gabriel's first solo LP, *Peter Gabriel*, which, inevitably, rose high in the charts. The belief that money can make anyone a star is probably unfounded. Usually a group will have achieved some local popularity in pub, club or dance hall before an enterprising manager or A and R man picks them up. But without commercial backing, the climb to the top is impossible. The manipulative role of the manager or agent (Epstein, Oldham, Grossman) is crucial. And the record contract is the gateway to success for any aspiring group. Without it there is no media exposure, only the routine grind round halls and clubs.

So the bargaining position of an unknown group is very weak. In return for the promotion and the possibility of stardom, the companies will probably have total control over the musical lives and even the personal lives of the performers. The music, after all, is only part of the product. To achieve the correct image, hair may be cut, or allowed to grow long, sideburns shaved, names changed, clothes overhauled, teeth straightened. Women, naturally, are even more likely to be remodelled in order to fit the stereotype.

The star groups, established moneymakers, can make their own terms, control their own music, make their own records to sell to the major labels. But by the time they are rich and powerful there is no need for external pressures to make them conform to the winning image. The market forces are, as it were, internalised. And there is nothing much left for them to write about either – only narcissistic songs about the pain and loneliness of being rich and famous.

A group that fails to achieve an adequate return is made redundant. Money rules, particularly in times of economic squeeze.

The record industry has been contracting in recent years. Fewer records have been made and profits have been maintained by higher prices. The policy, certainly of the major labels, is to concentrate on predictable winners, established sellers, rather than gamble on unknowns. Smaller artists, smaller labels risk being squeezed out.

If the record companies control the manufacturing and marketing side of the industry, the music publishers control its 'creative' side. Copyright royalties – split equally between the publisher and the writer or writers – represent a major source of profit. Without the backing of a publisher, a songwriter can make little headway in the business. And, again, the pressure is on him to find a winning formula or make way for someone who can.

Numerous other enterprises feed off the music industry. The pop-music papers, dependent for their revenue on advertisements from record companies, the dance halls, the discos, the manufacturers of T-shirts, posters and badges, the boutiques, the creators of teenage fashions constitute a mammoth industry, a conglomeration of companies all dedicated to making money out of music by giving the public what they want it to want. For socialist musicians to challenge this industry with their creativity and their music and still survive on their terms seems to me as likely as walking on the water in a thunderstorm.

As for the product itself, it is convenient, and it may even be accurate, to divide the cesspool of popular music into two streams. One is manufactured within the industry itself by the professionals of Tin Pan Alley or Denmark Street, hack writers with rhyming dictionaries, an ear for the latest trend and a facility for turning out cheerfully empty ditties or banally sentimental ballads. The heyday of the professionals was in the 1920s and 1930s in the States, when Cole Porter, Oscar Hammerstein II and Jerome Kern, Rodgers and Hart, the Gershwin brothers were crafting the songs that they hoped approximated to high art and that are now the standards drooled over by the 'they-don't-write-them-like-that-any-more' brigade.

Certainly they were skilfully made, used complex chord structures, worked in clever and unlikely rhymes. They were deft and sophisticated and flattered the egos of the elegant set at Broadway musicals and smart nighclubs. But they do not bear too close inspection. They have no substance. They break easily. And they lie about the America of that time. While Harbach and Kern were writing 'Smoke Gets In Your Eyes' and the very rich Cole Porter was producing 'Night and

Day' for the cafe society glamour girls and men about town, children were dying in their thousands of TB, pellagra or just plain starvation. The Alley's only acknowledgement of the Depression was the tear-jerking sentiment of 'Buddy Can You Spare A Dime?'.

The other stream of popular music bubbles up, as it were, from below. Music that springs from and is part of the life of a community, with its own recognisable identity, idiom and culture – ghetto blacks, white hillbillies – is sucked in by the machine, watered down, sweetened up and generally processed to make it socially respectable and fit for consumption by a more cultivated audience with the money to pay for it. Grassroots music, as the Americans like to call it, is dressed up as showbiz. Most of the numbers of nameless musicians whose creativity nourished the hit parade were not professionals in the strict sense. Their music was organic, a way of coping with death, bad times and survival in a world where they had nothing. Chopped away from its roots, the property of the professionals and the businessmen, it becomes an accretion, something decorative, music to entertain, soothe, thrill.

This has been the recurring pattern in popular music from ragtime to rock'n'roll and at all stages in between. Anyone who suggests that it is possible to make music within the system, retaining control so that it does not become packaged entertainment, will be hard put to it to find any evidence that it has ever happened. Certainly before 1956 there is none at all. The relationship of musicians to businessmen has been strictly that of servants to masters.

The rock'n'roll revolution of the last twenty years did change that. For the first time performers and audience shared a common identity. The growth of a distinctive teenage audience with its own purchasing power, musical tastes and life-style was not in itself a threat to the music establishment. On the contrary, it provided a wonderful new market ripe for exploitation by a boom economy. The discontent of the young was real enough but it was skimmed off, processed and sold back to them as a teenage rebel package, an image that the teenagers then felt bound to live up to. Early rock'n'roll was sexy, raw, aggressive and sounded different from what the professionals and the manipulators and the media men were used to; but neither in its content nor in its structure did it present any challenge to their power. A nice reminder of that is the fact that the song that became a kind of anthem of teenage rebellion and led to a steady flow of ripped-up cinema seats – 'Rock Around The Clock' – was actually written by two professional songwriters whose combined ages totalled about a hundred.

Far more of a threat was the skiffle explosion, a purely British phenomenon, though its songs were mostly American – cotton-picking ballads, prison songs, Leadbelly, Guthrie – and it was a threat because it was technically so simple that anyone who could master a few guitar chords, thimble a washboard or plonk a one-string tea-chest bass could join in. You did not need to be a professional; in fact it helped if you were not, and it was happening in streets and cellars and pub rooms and coffee bars and on CND marches and everywhere outside the protection of the pop-music mafia. It was too limited to develop much and the money men soon bought over the Cliff Richards and Adam Faiths and Tommy Steeles. But it did lay the basis for much of what happened later in popular music, particularly the folk-club movement and the rhythm-and-blues movement. And by demystifying technique and breaking down the great divide between performers and audience, it offered just a blurred glimpse of a situation where the music is not the property of an elite but a shared experience in which everyone, in a sense, is a participant.

Despite the energy and creativity and spontaneity of individual musicians, it is difficult to believe, looking back over the last twenty years, that the structure of rock music has ever seriously challenged the values of the music business within which, by virtue of its expensive technology and high overheads, it is forced to operate. There are perhaps two movements which promised to break the commercial stranglehold but were finally defeated. One was the folk–protest movement – not in Britain, where protest was never anything but an artificially manufactured boom, but in the States, where protest to use the commercial label, was a genuine response, taking its idiom from the folk revival and its energy from the civil rights movement and the disaffection of the young with the Vietnam war. The fact that it was turned into a trend, a sound that lasted all of six months, does not invalidate that. But it does suggest that there was something about the singers and the songs which allowed them to be swallowed up by the music-biz monster with scarcely a hiccup.

Certainly many of the songs were little more than balloons with slogans scrawled on them and nothing inside. The ones that made the hit parade – 'Blowing In The Wind', 'If I Had A Hammer' (which dated back to 1950, when it was a different song), 'The Times They

Are A-changing' – were vague liberal sentiments that had little bite.
Out of context, removed from their social base and transformed into
media fodder, these songs were harmless – as they always will be.
But there were more specific songs that probed deeper – some of
Dylan, a few of Ochs and Paxton. The anti-establishment, anti-
Vietnam-war stand was genuine enough. Yet that whole movement
was painlessly absorbed, appropriated by the establishment in a way
that one cannot imagine happening to the first folk revival in the
1930s and 1940s. Woody Guthrie and Molly Jackson never became
stars, as Dylan and Baez did, nor were their songs launched into mass
circulation. But the revival of the 1930s was not about personalities;
that of the 1960s certainly was. The 1930s revival was rooted in the
working class and the union struggles; that of the 1960s in the
students and middle class, who carried little weight politically. The
songs of Molly Jackson and Guthrie were representative, they spoke
for their class and they knew which side they were on (Guthrie's
private life was never, as far as I know, turned into anguished songs);
Dylan's comment on the old certainties was, 'That's such a waste. I
mean, which side *can* you be on?'[1]

The songwriters of the 1960s expressed their individual feelings.
Their loyalty was to themselves, not to a class, not to a cause. Phil
Ochs stated: 'I'm only singing about my feelings, my attitudes, my
views.'[2] In the end, all Dylan had left to guide him was the feeling that
he must be true to himself and his art. 'I'm not part of no movement'
he said.[3] Their view of themselves made it easy for the image to
obscure the politics. And when that happens, what the song is about
hardly matters any more. The focus of attention is shifted from
content to charisma. Issues are personalised. Dylan, of course, aided
this process, denying that he spoke for anyone but himself, disowning
his protest songs, withdrawing into the dreamlike imagery of his
private fantasies; then – like any rock star – going electric. It was less
a question of selling out than a process of adaptation and adjustment,
of surviving the unreality and isolation of success.

The other spontaneous eruption of popular music in the 1960s
happened on the West Coast. Rock music was the natural expression
of the student–hippie community of the Bay area. It was the
alternative culture, it was peace and love, it was doing your own
thing. It was community control and the battle for the People's Park
in Berkeley. It was hostility towards the war in Vietnam and the
commercial values of straight Amerika. It was rejection of the

institution of marriage and the work ethic. It was sex and drugs as a voyage of self-discovery. All very subversive. The music, fusing rock, folk and the Beatles, was, at the outset, created from within the community and controlled by the musicians themselves. Some of it was overtly political, notably that of Country Joe and the Fish.

Yet within a year or two the alternative culture was big business, the musicians were bought into superstardom by lucrative record contracts, aging hacks were churning out silly songs about flowers, the message 'liberate your minds' turned out to be both politically safe and eminently saleable, and the trappings, flowers, bells, beads, kaftans and psychedelic paraphernalia had become an industry. The guerrillas had simply, without their even realising it, been incorporated into the regular army of the enemy. The political naivety of the hippie ideology, their isolation from the real world and inability to understand the power structure of the society they were rejecting, the increasing incapacity of the successful musicians to distinguish between media illusion and reality – witness John Lennon's curious belief that you could achieve peace through publicity – and their apparent unawareness of the contradiction between their professed beliefs and their actual role as luminaries of the system – all this made the defeat of the dream inevitable. And as long as rock depends on expensive technology, and as long as that technology and the production processes are controlled by businessmen, all such dreams are doomed.

Yet control of technology is only one problem in rock music. The nature of the idiom itself is the other. The message of rock music is that the words do not matter. The style matters, the froth, the bubbles, the colours, the lights, the clothes, the charisma, the sound, the bodily movements, the beat – these matter. The words don't matter. Any significance the words may attempt to carry is inevitably defeated by that message. The most rock can hope to communicate – as with punk rock – is simple-minded slogans. Frank Zappa: 'Involvement derives essentially from the music itself and not from the lyrics. For me the words are just a carefully manufactured part of the packaging medium of the music. The words are more relevant to the album cover than they are to the songs.'[4] Mick Jagger explained his mumbling during songs as being a means of covering over the bad lines. The lyrics are not that important to him, though he makes an exception, of course, for the hook line, which is often the only line you can hear. Pop critic Richard Williams, writing in *Melody Maker* about a funky Italian singer, made this astonishing declaration:

> I've listened to all these five albums many times now, some over a
> period of years, and I've yet to understand a word of the lyrics. It
> doesn't matter a damn. What Battisti has to say communicates
> above linguistic barriers.[5]

He did not, though, anywhere in the article enlighten us as to what
Battisti does have to say. Nor did he find it relevant to mention the
fact that Battisti donates a percentage of his record royalties to a neo-
fascist party.

Rock is a sound, its structure is predictable, its idiom is mindless. It
is incapable of laughter, it is incapable of development. It inhabits an
unreal world in which everything is for show. Deprived of the
sharpness, the stimulus, the subtlety, the allusiveness, the explosive-
ness of words, rock relies on volume and repetition to generate
excitement. Yet, despite its surface energy, nothing actually happens
in rock music, which is the most reassuring thing about it. Rock's
sexism has often been pointed out, but that sexism seems to me to be
part and parcel of a music that, in style, in mode of performance and
sometimes in content, is fascist, obsessed with the elevation of
supergods for the adoration of the passive multitudes.

The argument that to reach people you have to use the popular
music form is spurious. It confuses numbers in the market place with
people. It ignores the quality of the communication and the
relationship between audience and performer. More, it ignores the
fact that rock is an exclusive music and that the range of concerns and
emotions expressed in it is extraordinarily small and largely adoles-
cent. Like any commodity in the market, purchase of it buys entry to
an exclusive group. It is incapable of saying anything valuable about
the world in which most people live, love and work. At best it ignores
their concerns, their feelings; at worst it expresses open contempt for
their ordinariness, their old-fashionedness, their utter failure to make
it, their lives so dull, plastic and meaningless in comparison to the
glamour, excitement and significance of the world of pop stardom.
Rock erects walls of sound within which the young can feel free.
Outside there is nothing. A generation is annihilated.

It may not be true in fact, but it would certainly be appropriate as a
metaphor that when the generals took over in Chile they blasted rock
music through the loudspeakers into the streets of Santiago – cultural

violence reflecting political and economic violence. The indigenous music was stifled and its practitioners arrested, killed and exiled.

What, then, is the alternative? The folk-club circuit and the folk idiom have to be taken seriously as possibilities to build on, because they have exactly those strengths lacking in the commercial music world. Folk clubs in Britain – mainly because of the accident that pub rooms can be hired without the landlords or the breweries exercising any control – are controlled by the local organisers and the locally-based audience. There are no business interests involved; no one profits. A folk club has the makings of a community-controlled meeting place for live music. Moreover the structure of a folk-club evening is essentially democratic. The guest performer comes out of, is not physically or in status separate from, the audience. There is generally no amplification. Communication is based on the spoken word rather than the shouted sound. Glamour and image play little part. Floor singers and audience participation are encouraged.

The content of a folk-club evening is something else. Songs may be chosen with little regard for contemporary relevance. Participation may be exalted at the expense of content. Recent years have seen the growing popularity of songs which escape into a romanticised world of pastoral innocence. There is a highly reactionary strand of romantic nationalism in the folk movement. Songs are still seen as decorative rather than functional. Folk purists are bent on turning the music into a museum exhibit, to be dusted down and admired once a week, untouched by the outside world.

But this is far from what the modern folk revival had in mind in its early years. This revival – in America in the 1930s and in Britain in the 1950s – redefined folk song. The first collectors, at the beginning of this century, saw folk song as a survival from the past, peasant song, the spontaneous expression of communities unaffected by literacy, commerce or industry. Redefined, folk song becomes, to quote A. L. Lloyd, 'the musical and poetic expression of the fantasy of the lower classes – and by no means exclusively the country workers.'[6] In short, it reflects the world as seen by those at the bottom. Consequently its heroes and heroines are rarely the great men and women of history books but transported poachers, press-ganged ploughboys, beggars and deserters, law-breakers and machine-wreckers, female highwaymen, pitmen, millgirls and servant girls. At its best it asserts subversive qualities – a sturdy independence, disrespect for social conventions, defiance of authority, frankness about sex, loyalty to friends and loved ones rather than to country, and a marked lack of enthusiasm for the puritan ethic. And it has stirring within it a longing for a better life. Because words are paramount, because as redefined it now incorporates industrial ballads and topical songs, it does have the potential for social change that no other idiom at the moment can offer.

There is, then, a considerable body of music, song and dance – variable in quality, it is true, but spanning a wide range of emotions and experiences, the cultural wealth of a class from whom it has been taken as the material wealth they have produced has been taken, yet still surviving in some form or other in pockets of Ireland, Scotland and even England. The question is: should this music become the property of antiquarians – 'relic specialists' – or could it be a living part of the everyday lives and struggles of working people? And if the latter, how are these songs to be disseminated, absorbed into the mainstream of a life in which the time and space for singing are severely restricted, and in the face of the dominant song imposed by the pop business?

One answer has been to go electric and compete in the market place. But electric backing will not in itself make a folk song contemporary or relevant; it may embalm it as rigidly as a stylised performance in a folk club. Another answer came out of the American experience of unionisation. Song, Wobbly parodies, union anthems, topical ballads, became a useful weapon in the context of an open and often violent conflict between workers and bosses. The forging of links between the ideology of northern radical intellectuals and the militancy of southern textile and mine workers gave rise to – something rare in the British tradition – politically conscious songs in the traditional idiom and provided the impetus for the folk revival that followed. The Almanac Singers, formed at the end of the 1930s, strove 'to make and sing songs however and whenever they are needed in the workers' struggle'. The effectiveness of the Almanacs and of People's Songs after them was limited by the political climate of the times – the Cold War and anti-Communist witch-hunt – and by the attachment they had to a party line. This model, seemingly inapplicable in the 'I'm-not-part-of-no-movement' 1960s, has been revived by the agit-prop theatre groups in the 1970s.

It seems possible that the folk clubs could be broadened to take on the role of servicing the political needs of their community. But it can hardly be claimed that this has yet happened. And the folk revival has not really succeeded in throwing up a coherent body of contemporary song relevant to people's needs. It will be argued that this is because the folk idiom itself is now archaic, remote from the experience of, say, Halewood car workers or Hackney housewives. Partly it may be true, or true of one part of the tradition. Yet when the *Sunday Times* ran a competition for the best song written about a sporting hero, not one of the thousand entries received used the rock idiom or even the more middle-of-the-road pop ballad. Three-quarters of them used what could loosely be described as a folk or broadside ballad idiom, set to tunes such as 'Villeykins and His Dinah'. Clearly, when people have a need to express themselves on any subject other than teenage love, they find no useful model in the rock or pop idiom. The folk tradition, though perhaps at its most doggerel, is still found to be serviceable.

The problem of idiom is obviously crucial. And it is a problem of finding not an idiom *through* which the specialist can reach or convert the masses but one *in* which people can find their own voice and express their own experiences and perceptions of society. Songs never converted anyone. That is not what they are for. They are for sharing – ideas, hopes, feelings about what is sad, funny, ridiculous, horrifying. They are for making a community of the already converted.

Chapter 4

The Struggle for Song: a Reply to Leon Rosselson

Gary Herman and Ian Hoare

The old-fashioned 'artist' – let us call him the author . . . must see it as his goal to make himself redundant as a specialist . . . His social usefulness can best be measured by the degree to which he is capable of using the liberating factors in the media and bringing them to fruition. The tactical contradictions in which he must become involved in the process can neither be denied nor covered up in any way. But strategically his role is clear. The author has to work as the agent of the masses. He can lose himself in them only when they themselves become authors, the authors of history.[1]

The Marxist vision of history shows it to be the totality of struggle. At any given historical conjuncture the revolutionary must be prepared to take up the struggle wherever productive contradictions arise. And they arise not only in the spheres of material production and political organisation, but with equal significance in the spheres of ideological production and cultural life.

Of all the ideological forms – or kinds of 'spiritual production', as Marx puts it – which flourish in bourgeois society, music and particularly song seems to present revolutionaries with the greatest problems.[2] While it is the most accessible of all kinds of ideological production, song is also, as Leon Rosselson points out, at the centre of a billion-dollar industry – the record business.

The record is a type of commodity specific to late capitalism, but the song retains links with an earlier stage of social development. Captured on record, the song becomes a commodity to be transformed into profit for the industry. The singer who works for a record company (or the songwriter dependent on publishers for income) becomes a productive labourer, exploited and expropriated – notwithstanding the rare attainment of rich rewards. Thus singer and song straddle two worlds uncomfortably – on the one hand there are vast conglomerates like EMI, Philips and CBS; on the other there are ceilidhs, folk clubs, friendly jam sessions or even bath-tub soloists. The technology of mechanical reproduction has, as Walter Benjamin says, 'transformed the entire nature of art'[3] – and, therefore, of song. But the old nature of song as popular expression rooted in the experience of the oppressed classes has not been destroyed by this transformation.

The revolutionary must be engaged in the struggle to politicise song. This can be seen as one part of a wider struggle to 'return art to the people', in William Morris's felicitous phrase.[4] In other words, the revolutionary must counter the persistent attempts of the bourgeois media, the record companies, radio stations and so on to expropriate ideological products and ideological production. But he or she does not start from scratch in this struggle – even if it is fought under conditions determined by capitalism itself.

Rosselson has adequately demonstrated that songs have played a political role as agit-prop even in recent times. They have also given expression to the oppressed, down-trodden and exploited. A good proportion of recorded music does that too. As Rosselson himself acknowledges, there is a stream of popular music that 'bubbles up from below'. Media companies might transmit songs and produce records of them, but the songs themselves are produced by workers within the industry or people outside it. Manipulation is a one-sided and inaccurate description of the operations of the media in this field. There is an important contradiction stemming from the record companies' need the expropriate the ideological products of a popular culture or subculture in order to reproduce them for exchange. This contradiction is specific to a society which mass markets ideological products, and it is at its most acute where song is concerned.

There is a two-way relationship between the production of songs and the production of records. Not only do record companies expropriate ideological products and transform them, but the companies' products can themselves be transformed by the culture which receives them. A record may have one meaning determined by the social relations of its production – but its meaning is also affected by the social relations underlying its consumption. Because records are interpreted, because they stimulate song, their consumption is not merely passive.

The dominant ideology may be reinforced in consumption, but it is equally capable of being undermined. The Strawbs' 'Part Of The Union', intended as a direct attack on trade unionism, achieves quite the reverse effect when sung (or just sung-along-to) by Coventry car workers. A song's meaning is not immutable, independent of context. One of the most familiar examples of effect of context on meaning is seen among football crowds. A trite Tin Pan Alley ballad like 'You'll Never Walk Alone' is taken up by the fans at Liverpool and becomes an anthem of solidarity. Football crowds are also well known for freely adapting all kinds of songs and music. 'Land of Hope and Glory' becomes 'We Hate Nottingham Forest'. An American pop instrumental hit by the Routers ('Let's Go') is the source of one of the most common rhythms heard on the terraces at any football match.

The folk tradition is full of such adaptation. The Wobblies, and especially Joe Hill, knew about this and gave new words to old hymns – turning songs of Christian resignation into numbers like 'Dump the Bosses off Your Back'. It is a mistake to believe that the products of the record companies are any less susceptible to critical intelligence. A record only becomes an ideological product proper when it is played and becomes song. At that point it is a raw material which can be moulded by context and adaptation. In fact, it is a mistake to believe that you can totally separate ideological consumption from ideological production.

As Rosselson states, popular music has undergone a number of significant changes in the past two or three decades. Rock'n'roll, folk–protest, reggae and punk have all left their mark. Their impact has not been revolutionary in itself – but then, Marxists do not expect ideological products to bring about that sort of change. We would not imagine that the directors of EMI might plump for socialism just because the Beatles stop selling records. They will, of course, simply look for the next big seller, building on the changes – in song style, manufacturing methods and marketing technique – that did accompany the Beatles.

These changes have a sound economic basis. The record companies' implacable search for profit cannot afford to ignore the grass-roots of popular song – the amateur or semi-pro musicians who perform in small clubs or pub rooms, or, for that matter, the kinds of music that audiences want and will often create if they cannot buy them. Nor is the music business a monolithic institution. All record companies operate according to marketing decisions, but it is one of the specific features of the music business that there are different markets, different marketing techniques and different kinds of product worth marketing. In a sense all records are the same, because they are all results of the same process of material production. But this offers us another productive contradiction. Because they are the same, to a large extent it does not matter what is in the grooves – as long as it sells. In the absence of complete state control of record production, distribution and technology, there is always the possibility of alternative voices making themselves heard.

The Sex Pistols have provided recent evidence of this. Despite actual censorship by radio stations and record companies – and, in the case of one album, harassment by the law – 'God Save The Queen' and *Never Mind The Bollocks, Here's The Sex Pistols* both became best-sellers. Clearly, the industry selects the ideological products it seeks to expropriate, but it does not operate as a unit and the criteria for selection are flexible.

Rosselson asserts not only that the present output of the media is more or less uniformly worthless and bound to remain so, but in particular that politically committed artists should themselves avoid getting involved in the industry. Since record companies are capitalist, the argument runs, the subversive power of the work of revolutionary artists will inevitably be undermined. In one form or another this argument has a respectable pedigree – A. L. Lloyd,[5] Ewan MacColl and the Park House Convention [6] have all defended folk music in terms similar to Rosselson's. Indeed, the position bears some similarity to that of critics, commentators and artists who have seen in the growth of the mass media a kind of creeping vulgarity.

Let us accept that there is a 'threatened species' of politically valuable song stemming from folk music and unlikely to flourish in the corridors of EMI. This implies that there is useful work to be done by socialist performers, writers and others in keeping that tradition alive at a grassroots level. But it does not follow that the only fitting response to the mass media is to abandon them. The media won't go away if we ignore them, any more than radical songs alone will bring capitalism to its knees.

Clearly the committed singer–writer has to battle against great odds if she or he enters the mainstream of the music business. But the failure of so-called 'alternative' cultures to survive within the record industry is no reason to condemn them as fruitless – just as the fact that the Co-op is now one of the biggest traditional retailers in the market is no reason to condemn the Rochdale pioneers as misguided. There are vitally important struggles to be taken up in the field of the mass media, initially for access, ultimately for control. 'The temptation to withdraw is great', as Enzensberger says of a similar case, when the record company can advertise 'The revolution is on CBS'. But, as Enzensberger concludes, 'fear of handling shit is a luxury a sewerman cannot necessarily afford.'[7]

The radical folk argument very often takes the form of a diatribe against the supposedly stultifying and elitist character of rock. Rosselson suggests, for instance, that rock cannot have genuinely popular roots because of its 'expensive technology and high overheads'. But the investment required to launch a rock band may not be quite as forbidding an obstacle as he seems to imply. For every piece of expensive new technology there is a piece of cheap old technology: second-hand tape machines, for instance, or Woolworths electric guitars (recommended by punks) which are probably cheaper than Rosselson's own acoustic. It is also worth noting that the emergence of large numbers of British beat groups in the early 1960s followed closely on the introduction of hire purchase.

But the complaint about the technology of rock is not merely one of inaccessibility. Rosselson's position ultimately makes no distinction between the function of the technology under capitalism and its potential under popular control. The use of electrical equipment in music is itself seen as suspect on the primarily aesthetic grounds that it has led merely to a loud, violent music which would be a fit weapon for the Chilean fascists.

The political dangers of a blind cultural archaism taking over here are evident. Advances in the technology available to music-makers create *new* aesthetic and political possibilities. The revolutionary response cannot be a sweeping dismissal of these because of the form they have tended to take under capitalist control. In some situations even the megaphone that Rosselson apparently despises can be a socialist weapon; and it is politically irresponsible to recommend on principle that songs are kept, as it were, in cotton wool, unsoiled by the mechanical hardware needed for amplification and mass reproduction. There are pressing questions to be considered not only about how to gain control of that technology but about ways of modifying it to meet popular needs, and ways of exploring its potential. Indeed, as Marx, Lenin and Trotsky have all argued, socialism *demands* technological advance; technology lies at the foundation of culture, and 'the decisive instrument in the cultural revolution must be a revolution in technique'.[8]

Part of the problem with the radical folk argument is that it tends to transform an evaluation of a particular genre into a position on music in general, without noticing some of the crucial questions which are thereby overlooked. Thus rock is dismissed because its noisiness presents an insurmountable obstacle to the 'communication' – primarily verbal and intimate – which Rosselson rightly sees as the great strength of the folk tradition. But such criteria are, of course, totally irrelevant to instrumental and electronic music; and rock itself does not consist solely or even principally of songs. When Rosselson attacks rock musicians for saying 'the words don't matter', is he suggesting that *only* the words matter, that music itself is ideologically neutral and has no 'content'? By these guidelines, the black nationalist movement in jazz would presumably be meaningless at best and possibly even reactionary. It is true that 'style' is a vital consideration in rock and in the entire Afro-American tradition; and the act of recording the music underlines this, since a particular *performance* is captured for reproduction. But does this preoccupation with style imply cultural emptiness? Or could it be that the stylistic attributes themselves convey meaning, understood by reference to their cultural contexts? Symptomatically, Rosselson has little to say about the importance of dance in popular music.

Rosselson's revulsion at the aesthetics of rock leads to political confusion at several points. It is argued, for example, that a key weakness of the rock performers of the 1960s was their preoccupation with 'personal feelings' – Woody Guthrie is praised for never singing about his private life. But we must surely recognise that no aspect of life can be excluded from a revolutionary critique. Can't a woman's song about her own marriage be politically significant? Trotsky and Breton, for whom 'all true art' was revolutionary, argued that is was imperative that 'the artist . . . freely seeks to give his own inner world incarnation in his art'.[9]

Neither is there anything inherent in the rock genre as such to prevent its lyrics dealing with whatever subject the writer chooses. Indeed, a large proportion of rock songs of the 1960s were notable for their social rather than their private orientation – the Kinks, the Who, John Lennon, Chuck Berry, the Mothers of Invention, Country Joe and Jefferson Airplane provide some of the more obvious examples. The same is true of a substantial part of soul music in the USA, from Curtis Mayfield through Marvin Gaye to Gil Scott-Heron. And Jamaican pop music has been increasingly social in outlook in the 1970s – how can we disregard the existence of such reggae songs as the Revolutionaries' 'MPLA' or Johnny Clarke's 'Freedom Fighters'?

The failure to take account of the history of contemporary black music also indicates an incipient parochialism in the radical folk argument, and a seriously limited conception of who the proletariat are. The folk song tradition outlined by Rosselson in no sense belongs to the thousands of West Indian car workers in Dagenham. There are precious few white workers left in the cotton mills, so much a part of A. L. Lloyd's folk milieu. And to dismiss rock or pop by labelling it 'cultural imperialism' is not good enough. Capitalist exploitation crosses national and cultural boundaries. So must the socialist response. And the internationalism of the mass media provides another of its productive contradictions.

Rosselson's failure to recognise contradictions in the music industry leads him to ignore fruitful possibilities for revolutionary theory and practice. Confronted with capitalist domination in the sphere of ideological production, his strategy is to abandon the struggle there for fear of defeat – to withdraw from the market place and ask, 'What is the alternative?' But there are no alternatives in Rosselson's sense. Even his own practice does not escape capitalism. The question we should be asking is not 'What is the alternative?' but 'What is to be done?' Marxism advocates a conjunctural struggle in which there are no moral imperatives and no historical absolutes; and the potential of that struggle cannot be delimited in advance.

To say that we have to return song to the people is not to present a *solution* to the problem of politicising song. It is, on the contrary, a

statement of the revolutionary aim. In seeking to achieve this goal
revolutionaries are fighting against capitalist appropriation on every
level – not against a particular kind of ideological production but
against the all-pervasive *form* of ideological production. The fact that
there are people who will listen to radical songs in certain venues is
not an anomaly or an exception within capitalism, but part of its
contradictory nature.

Rosselson's proposition, however, is that left political song needs a
refuge of 'non-capitalism' in order to survive at all. The audience he
envisages is 'already converted' to revolutionary politics and is thus
held to be outside capitalism. He even suggests venues for the
political singer or musician – pub rooms – which he claims are
beyond the grasp of the capitalists who run the brewery industry.

Of course, pub rooms are *not* a no-man's land in the class war.
Nor is it merely accidental that the songs sung in those rooms display
'a highly reactionary strand of romantic nationalism' and have 'little
regard for contemporary relevance' – as Rosselson himself admits.
Rosselson's argument avoids asking crucial questions about the real
nature of song in a bourgeois society and comes up with a fiction that
suits his particular aspirations as a performer.

There is no doubt that left political song can be sheltered in the
rarified atmosphere of political meetings and radical folk clubs; but,
like over-protected children, it will fail to grow in that environment.
Art and artist will become politically neutered by following the route
into a political by-way. The argument is, in the end, a prescription for
keeping the political struggle against capitalism external to musical
practice itself.

Marxism does not guarantee victory in each and every partial
struggle. But Marxism is neither fatalist nor defeatist. It cannot
retreat from the ideological front and still remain a weapon in the
struggle to overthrow capitalism. If some battles *appear* to be
unwinnable that is all the more reason for developing new strategies.
'On the ideological front . . .', Gramsci wrote, 'it is necessary to
engage battle with the most eminent of one's adversaries.'[10]

Leon Rosselson has been actively and creditably involved in
certain areas of ideological struggle for many years. Nonetheless,
there are other areas which Marxist theory and practice cannot
ignore. These areas call for a genuine critique of the music industry
and of music itself – a critique which can only develop hand in hand
with a struggle on all fronts.

We have begun to describe an industry whose major product –
recorded popular music, which Rosselson unhappily equates with a
particular kind of popular music known as rock – is at the heart of a
number of contradictions. These contradictions provide the basis of a
programme of action around different but connected aspects of the
production of song and music. No part of the struggle to 'return song
to the people' is independent of any other. Indeed, the ideological
struggle is, in a very real sense, a unity – and it is inseparable from the
struggle against capitalism. But there are certain objectives within the
reach of revolutionaries. Of course, these objectives fall short of the
seizure of state power by the proletariat – but they are part of the
same struggle. The objectives are:

1. The unionisation of all productive workers within the music
industry, including performers and songwriters.
2. The development of close links between music workers and
revolutionary organisations.
3. Access to, control over and, eventually, ownership of the means
of ideological production for the working class.
4. The utilisation of already available technology and technique
by revolutionary organisations and other radical groups, with the
aim, in particular, of making record production and distribution
available to revolutionary artists.
5. The encouragement of lyrical and musical experimentation in
order to free song and music from the strait-jacket of bourgeois
notions of acceptability and popularity and to develop progressive
musical idioms.
6. The establishment and encouragement of performance contexts
which challenge the commodity form of entertainment and the
conventional distinctions between audience and performer, consumer and producer.

There is already some activity directed towards these goals, though
probably not as much as is in publishing or film-making. Performers
like Henry Cow and Leon Rosselson himself have an invaluable role
to play. So too do organisations like Rock Against Racism, Music for
Socialism and their equivalents in other countries. Even the British
Musicians' Union has recently taken an enormous step forward by
admitting the need to unionise rock musicians. The struggle must be
extended and developed and Marxism can play a crucial role in the

determination of realistic strategies. For, as Dave Laing has noted, 'the question is not *whether* to work inside or outside the established cultural institutions, but *how* to work inside or outside them'.[11]

Chapter 5

Political Theatre and the Working Class

Chris Rawlence

In periods of economic crisis, art has a tendency to concern itself more with politics. It was true of the 1930s and it has been true of the period since 1968. Politicised by the times, many artists, writers, musicians and performers have felt the need to express this commitment through their work.

Since 1968 there has been a development in theatre which embodies this political–cultural commitment. It consists of several dozen small independent theatre companies whose intention has been to define a new audience for theatre with a new kind of material. The new audience is a primarily working-class audience as opposed to the prevailing middle-class and 'theatre-going' audience of the established theatre. The new material consists of plays and shows which take as their raw material the lives, struggles, aims and aspirations of these contemporary audiences. They are mainly touring companies. They take their work to their audiences and tend to avoid theatres. Most are full-time, with a high proportion of Equity membership. After a long and continuing campaign, many are subsidised by the Arts Council, although the level of subsidy is felt by most companies to be inadequate. None of the companies is attached to a political party, yet most have a broadly socialist outlook.

Among these theatre companies are 7:84 (England and Scotland), Belt and Braces, Red Ladder, Broadside, Counteract, Roadgang,

Women's Theatre Group, Monstrous Regiment, Banner, Live Theatre, Theatremobile, M6, Recreation Ground, Common Stock, North West Spanner, CAST, Mutable, The Combination, Half Moon, Pirate Jenny, Foco Novo, Avon Touring, Gay Sweatshop, Interplay, a number of theatre-in-education teams, and at times the offspring touring theatre companies of the regional arts associations – for example, Emma, Solent Song and Dance, and Pentabus.

These companies are often lumped together as part of the 'fringe' or 'alternative' theatre. But these are confusing terms which obscure important differences between these and other so-called 'fringe' companies. Attempts to find a suitable description of the work have so far included 'socialist theatre' – which, accurate though it may be, has the disadvantage of appearing too political for 'non-political' audiences, thus keeping them away; 'popular theatre' – which is too vague; and 'community theatre' – which is rapidly gaining currency with funding bodies and which is based on companies' choice of venue and audience.

The notes that follow are an attempt to air some of the questions and problems raised by the work of the community/socialist theatre companies. They come largely out of my experience of ten years' work with Red Ladder Theatre. They are not posed as definitive assertions but as a means of taking the discussion further.

Why Theatre?

When the photograph came along painters had to ask: why painting? When good reproductions came along they asked again: not simply why, but what? With film and television, theatre workers face the same question: why theatre? Trevor Griffiths and Ken Loach do it pretty well on television: they reach millions with their plays and films in a single evening, and very effectively. The 'man with the movie camera' can go anywhere, show anything. So we have seriously to ask ourselves, what can a small theatre group do in Wigan Labour Club that television or a good film could never do?

It is true that at present the community theatre groups have a greater freedom to express opinions from a socialist standpoint than do socialists working in film or television. The latter are subject to much tighter political controls and censorship from above. But this is not a permanent distinction: it might change either way with a change in the political climate; grant-giving bodies have the power of political censorship in their ability to withhold subsidy. At the time of writing, North West Spanner are facing just such a problem with the tory-controlled management board of North West Arts Association.

In one sense theatre is more flexible than film. It requires no complex shooting procedure or editing for a final print. It can respond at all stages to events whereas the finality of a film cannot. Videotape is more flexible, but it has the disadvantage, in relation to theatre, of requiring a complex technology. But these seem to be minor distinctions. Either there is something more fundamentally particular to theatre, or we are engaged in a quaintly outmoded cultural activity.

An essential part of a theatrical experience is the audience's collective awareness of itself as an audience. It is an awareness, when positive, that performers both create and depend upon. And it can usually occur only when the audience is above a certain size in relation to the size of the auditorium. Any good live performance is not just dependent on the performers' abilities to get skilfully through their piece: it depends upon performers moving individual members of the audience to move each other; and in this collective response of the audience, the performers are moved to a better performance. Good live performance involves a three-way relationship: between the spectator, other spectators, and the performers; it is the ever-changing result of continuous feedback between these three parties. In this sense a theatre audience can feel it has the power, collectively, to shape the performance: audience as much as performers create it. This is a potential quality of theatre that neither film nor television can achieve because they are not live.

Television shows to ones, twos and threes, often in family units. Its audience never has a sense of itself as an audience – only as individuals. Less still do viewers – a passive term – feel they have power to shape the image. Films, on the other hand, do show to large audiences. But the darkness of the auditorium, the large scale of the images, and – as with television – the spectators' inability to influence or change the images combine to isolate the members of the audience from one another, taking them passively and alone into the world of the film. The sense of collective is denied. The heckler in the cinema gives you a jump, reminding you of the presence of other people. The heckler in the theatre is simply an extension, approved or disapproved of, of the collective audience response that is expected of live performance. He/she is no surprise.

The collectivity of live performance is not, of course, particular to socialist theatre. All theatre can build on it, whatever its class orientation. But it does have certain political implications for socialists.

Raymond Williams has suggested a definition of working-class culture: 'The crucial distinguishing element in English life since the Industrial Revolution is . . . between alternative ideas of the nature of social relationship . . . what is properly meant by "working-class culture" . . . is the basic collective idea, and the institutions, manners, habits of thought, and intentions which proceed from this'[1] (as opposed to middle-class ideas about individualism).

Capitalism collectivised the working class at the point of production during the Industrial Revolution. Collectivity, imposed upon it, became its prime mode of defence – in the form of trade unions, Chartist lodges, co-operatives and so on – against the unemployment and wage-cutting of the capitalist system. The collectivism that it created became capitalism's worst enemy. Collectivism, mutuality and class solidarity have never been the only ideologies active within the working class, or we would have had socialism long ago. But they are still very much present in the working class today. As such they are still anathema to capitalism, which seeks by various means to destroy them. Whether it be the mass media's assault on the closed shop or its urging of the postal ballot in trade-union elections; whether it be the coercive pleas of the advertisers, pressurising us to buy this or that commodity to enhance our individual status over that of our neighbours – the message is always similar: competitive individualism is the prime mover; collectivity is at best idealistic and at worst undemocratic – 'a threat to society as we know it'.

Our theatre companies do not make working-class culture. But in being aware of both the collectivist aspirations of working-class culture on the one hand, and the potential that live performance has to create in an audience the feeling that it can collectively determine the outcome of the performance on the other, it is possible that we can act as a catalyst in reminding this audience of its own cultural and political potential.

Some Red Ladder History

Red Ladder began (in October 1968) by answering needs. The first shows were for tenants' associations in Tower Hamlets during the struggle against the GLC rent rises through 1968–9. We were asked to open meetings with sketches lasting five to ten minutes about the rent issue. The tenants wanted us to warm the meetings up, help build an atmosphere of solidarity and attract more people to the meeting. They were simple knockabout them-and-us pieces, starkly presenting the main issues in a stylistic mixture of student follies, panto and music hall. They were very popular and achieved what the organisers desired, playing sometimes to three packed tenants' meetings in a single evening. Soon the plays became more analytical, attempting with the same brevity and exuberance to explain more of the complexities of the developing rent struggle. In this way we tried to fuse entertainment with instruction.

These housing shows were also performed outdoors, mainly on demonstrations. Problems of visibility and audibility on noisy street corners led us to develop a highly visual outdoor style with text to a minimum.

By 1970 we were taking our shows into the trade-union movement. It was recognised by many shop stewards and other workers that theatre could fulfil an important educational function within their union. This involved invitations to Red Ladder to make and perform short plays about such questions as collective bargaining, the Industrial Relations Act, the role of advancing technology, the question of amalgamation in the AUEW, and unemployment. The venues for these shows were varied: car parks in the dinner-hour, and demonstrations; and for the indoor shows, trade-union weekend schools, meetings, work-ins and occupations. As with the tenants' shows, it was the functional nature of the work that organisers liked: they provided a very effective means of provoking thought and discussion around important issues for trade-union members. A play, with the discussion that usually followed, was often felt to be 'better than a thousand leaflets'. But the plays only succeeded because of the extreme care Red Ladder took over their construction: put together as a result of numerous discussions with workers, and visits to factories, the shows were from 15 to 40 minutes in length – short enough to open or close a meeting.

But the functional emphasis of these plays posed us with problems. At the outset of the play-making process we would reach a collective decision on what the play was to be about. We then sat down to argue out the politics, analyses, 'lines' that the play was to embody.

At the same time we wanted to present credible characters who went through a convincing development in the play. But in the process of making the play we often found that our 'correct analysis' stifled our ability to create living characters. They tended to become pop-up functions of competing points of view: puppetlike, they spouted correct or incorrect opinions. Awareness of this problem as the play emerged did not always enable us to overcome it: desperate attempts to humanise these political Frankensteins with injections of colloquiality and the odd joke failed. The term 'fleshing out' gained currency in the company, implying the overlaying of the skeletons of analysis with the meat of living people. But often political analysis and character development/characterisation were on such divergent courses by this time that no organic reconciliation was possible in the final text.

I am not arguing that political theatre should not have the function of stimulating thought and discussion, and it is important that the political thinking embodied in a piece of theatre that claims to be socialist is clear and consistent. But a number of political theatre groups, and their writers, share this tendency to over-analysis, which goes hand in hand with a misguided feeling of responsibility to 'get-it-all-in', leaving no issue untouched. A sure pointer to this tendency is when a company no longer describes its show as being *about*, say, unemployment, but as *dealing with* it. The play becomes a neat package of correctly processed analysis from which the imagination has been excluded. And without imagination there is little chance of good theatre.

Our next play – *A Woman's Work Is Never Done* (1973–4) – was about the position of working-class women at home and at work. Designed for labour movement audiences, its preparation entailed just as much analysis and discussion as previous plays had done: we argued out positions on the production and reproduction of labour power, on how men oppressed women, on nursery provision and on equal pay. But because these questions have a sexual–political core to them, there was less danger of analysis getting too far from basic questions of human relationships. As well as having lengthy discussions with working-class women about their experience, the women in the company brought to bear their own experience as women to the making of the play. These factors meant that less divergence of character/characterisation and political analysis occurred. Because of the women's movement, politics and drama were more successfully integrated.

With *A Woman's Work Is Never Done* Red Ladder began to widen the kind of audience it was looking for. We felt that a play which was about working people and sexual politics would have a much more popular appeal than a play about amalgamation in the AUEW.

Until 1973 we had been performing primarily in contexts set up by the organised labour movement. At these meetings, schools and demonstrations, the audience, while possibly swelled by the attraction of a play, were there for additional reasons – to vote on some important decision, express protest, hear a speaker or take part in some form of industrial action. In a sense they were for us a ready-made audience. During the 1970–4 period, millions of workers became involved in industrial and political struggle who had never been involved before. It was the time of the miners' strikes, the fight against the Industrial Relations Act, the Pentonville 5, and the struggle against Heath's Phases One, Two and Three. So our audiences through this period were not a 'converted' militant few: they were thousands of ordinary people seeking to protect their livelihoods by fighting unemployment and falling living standards. After 1974 there was a lessening of the struggle. Fewer people were actively involved. Fewer went to meetings. Our ready-made audiences began to dwindle to the 'committed' or 'converted' – although when it comes to sexual politics it is hard to speak of the 'converted'. We were faced with a choice: to make a political theatre for the politically conscious sector of the working class – those who continued to be actively involved; or to seek a broad working-class audience which would be attracted to our shows first and foremost because they offered the prospect of a good night out. We opted for the latter – the building of a popular socialist theatre, and the popular appeal of *A Woman's Work Is Never Done* helped us through this transition.

This new direction did not involve a complete change from past ways of working. With *It Makes You Sick* – the story of an engineer, his ulcer and the NHS – we combined working with a health-service unions (particularly NUPE, who organised tours of hospitals) with playing in the clubs and community halls of industrial communities where there was not necessarily a supporting labour movement structure. We have continued this dual approach, of working directly, as the night's entertainment, in working-men's clubs and of working within the structures of the labour movement, with our recent club shows – *Anybody Sweating?* and *Would Jubileeve It?* Our move to Yorkshire has enabled us to consolidate this dual approach on a regional basis. In this way we are seeking to become an organic part of the cultural life of a region.

Theatre and the Working Class

For many working-class people theatre is felt to be a culturally alien form of live entertainment. On the whole, plays are felt to be the concern of the middle class and the intelligentsia. A look at the artistic programmes of many repertory and national companies will tell us why: they consist largely of plays which are a long way removed from the lives and experience of working people. Ayckbourn's *Norman Conquests* is a good example: it was a hit in the West End and in a number of provincial reps, yet it did not, to my knowledge, attract substantial working-class audiences. It failed to do so – and maybe it never intended to do so – because at the play's centre were the lives of the middle class, whose life-styles, loves, worries and self-images were experienced by working-class people as 'other' – alien. Theatre is felt by the working class not just to be not about them, but also to be not for them: the prevailing policy of theatre managements to play safe, to cultivate and enlarge the middle-class audience, confirms them in this feeling. Theatre is felt as the terrain of another class. The ambience of many theatre buildings compounds this feeling: compared to the working-men's club or the local, they are special places whose decor and plush percolated hush is sometimes intimidating. A visit is sometimes felt as a pilgrimage to someone else's shrine. And there is often the problem of catching the last bus.

Sometimes provincial reps come up with exceptions to the rule. When the Sheffield Crucible put on *The Stirrings in Sheffield on Saturday Night* – about the knife-grinders' strike in the city during the 1860s – it was very popular with the working class of the city. The theatre organised to get that audience and succeeded. The Victoria, Stoke on Trent, has also been a consistent exception to the rule. But the overall pattern remains the same.

By making theatre about questions at the centre of the lives of working-class people – often in collaboration with them – and by performing this theatre in venues situated at or near the workplace or home, the community theatre companies have shown, through their popularity, that it is possible for theatre to develop a much broader audience. Venue is of key importance. It has been shown time and again, for the reasons outlined above, that arts centres, studio theatres, and the traditional theatres themselves will not attract working-class audiences of any significant size. On the other hand, it is the community centre, the concert room of the large labour club, the pub room, and at times the local college which are the successful venues for this popular theatre. For it is in these venues that the new audiences expect to enjoy themselves: it is here that their experience of live entertainment is rooted.

But even in appropriate venues the expectations of what theatre is – its middle-class associations – often creates wariness in a working-class audience about what it is going to see. In the end, it is the quality and relevance of the show that counts. But on the way, good publicity and organisation are essential in building this new audience.

In addition, the technical constraints of touring community theatre often serve to demystify and dethrone an audience's preconception of what theatre is. Each performance usually involves a separate set-up in a different hall or club. This places inevitable limits on the scale and complexity of sets and lighting. As the members of a company are seen by the audience carrying in rostra, light stands, trunks full of costume and props; as they are observed to one side, changing a costume during the show; as they are watched, and perhaps helped, dismantling, packing, and carrying out after the show; so they are seen and experienced by their audiences in the process of production. A working-class audience is an audience of producers. The revelation of means involved in this process of production presents theatre as work; performers are seen as workers; entertainers are seen as part of the world of production; cultural barriers are broken down – because the reality is that there often is a class barrier between the community theatre companies and the audiences they seek.

The social composition of the companies can be divided into roughly two groupings. Firstly there are a number of teachers, writers, artists and intellectuals; radicalised by 1968 and after, and many with a university background, they share a desire to fuse their politics with their work, choosing theatre as a means. Secondly, there are a large number of actors, actresses and other theatre workers who have 'defected' from established theatre; these are people who have been radicalised by high unemployment and oppressive working structures, but above all by the alienating futility of performing second-rate theatre to middle-class audiences. They sought an involvement in a kind of theatre that was more appropriate to their emergent socialist ideas.

Conspicuously absent from many of these theatre companies are people who have come directly from working-class backgrounds. While many may have originated from working-class backgrounds, these origins have often been filtered out by the middle-class milieu of higher education or the bourgeois cultural climate of established theatre. Probably the majority are from middle-class backgrounds and upbringings.

In a class sense, therefore, many of these companies approach their audiences from the outside. They are not immediately of the class and communities they wish to play for. It is consequently very easy to make errors of judgement in the writing and performance of shows if those involved are not very sensitive to the cultural and political consciousness of their audiences. And to gain this sensitivity there is no substitute for prolonged exposure to the values and world outlook of the audiences being written for and performed to. As an individual writer or a collective working on material, it is not sufficient to wrangle back and forth over this or that socialist analysis of a given issue and expect to distil from this abstract process a show that connects. A community theatre company must know its audiences.

Sometimes unnecessary barriers are set up by a theatre company emanating 'theatricality' on and around performances. For reasons of their own security and friendship, theatre workers often develop a manner of behaving with each other which is often felt by outsiders, if they experience it, to be exclusive, often in a class sense. I have argued that, to many working-class people, theatre is the cultural domain of the middle class; equally, theatricality in social behaviour – the darling-ing and public in-joking that sometimes gets out of hand – can confirm the prejudice felt against theatre.

Chapter 6

Class Strategies for a New Cinema

David Glyn

The decline in the British cinema has produced a set of class responses from various sources in and around the film industry. Here we shall look at the political relationship between these different programmes and stratagems. Certain conclusions may then be possible concerning the correct programme and demands for solving the crisis in the film industry from the standpoint of the working class, and the orientation which revolutionaries should have towards the various groups involved. Of particular concern, in this context, are the membership of the film workers' trade union – the Association of Cinematograph, Television and Allied Technicians (ACTT) – and certain sections of the 'independent' film-making milieu.

We are concerned with cinema as a specific apparatus incorporating production, distribution and exhibition. The 'film industry' refers here to practices relating to the cinema as such – excluding production for television and commercial production such as industrial promotions and advertising, but including 'independent' production on both commercial and non-commercial bases. in other words, this film industry is technically narrower than that embraced by 'Wardour Street' plus the studios, but aesthetically and politically broader than the commercial cinema. There is thus a polemical inclusion, in our definition of 'the cinema', of practices whose economic scale and nature leads to their being regarded as external to the 'film industry proper'. The inclusion results partly from a personal commitment to this 'other cinema'. More importantly, it derives from the conviction that cinema can be revived only through a break at every level – production, distribution, exhibition – from the profit-making imperatives which constrain the development of the capitalist industry, and that independent cinema is already practically implicated in that break.

The cinema as a whole is presently in dire economic straits. In the commercial sector 70 per cent of ACTT film workers are always unemployed and the number of cinema seats in circulation steadily diminishes. American productions consume a large proportion of domestic labour power while British capital generally settles for the direst commercial formulae. Capital investment has moved firmly against the reproduction of the cinema. We shall identify some of the causes of this after comparing conditions in the 'independent' sector with those just referred to in the commercial sector.

Many independent film-makers work commercially as freelancers but in their capacity as independents they are generally dependent on the state for financial support.[1] Production grants are dispensed by the British Film Institute Production Board and by regional arts associations. The BFI receives in excess of £2 million a year from the Department of Education and Science, of which £120,000 is available for film production. Only one in every thirty applicants for production awards is successful. The majority of independent film-makers spend most of their time seeking access to the means of production. The development of the independent sector of the cinema is painfully slow in consequence. The continuity of work which is vital to its evolution is lacking.

Thus it is clear that, in one respect at least, conditions in the commercial and independent sectors of the cinema are similar. In both spheres the producers are chronically separated from their means of production as a result of under-capitalisation. The reasons for this lack of finance, in both instances, can ·be discovered in the relations of production of capitalist society.

The Capitalist Causes of the Crisis in the Cinema

Capital's existence is premised and dependent upon the extraction of surplus value and its incorporation into capital at a sufficient rate. This process is not explicable in terms of the avaricious motivation of individual capitalists; it is the necessary condition of capitalism's existence. However, the means whereby individual capitals seek profit advantages over other capitals serves overall to reduce the rate at which surplus value is produced. The anarchic functioning of the economy leads to a tendency for the rate of profit to fall. Generalised economic crises recur whenever this tendency makes itself felt. The crisis is the form of capital's solution: it is the process whereby the fall in the rate of profit is offset. It involves an expansion of surplus value at the expense of labour. It is always, and necessarily, at the expense of the working class that 'normal' capitalist accumulation is re-established. Only a revolutionary political intervention by (and for) the working class can prevent that outcome.

In the context of the general crisis, competition between capitals and the quest for the most profitable spheres of investment intensifies. Unproductive and less productive capitals are destroyed in order that the overall rate of profit may increase. In the present conjuncture, feature-film production is an unattractive investment proposition. Moreover, unproductive state spending (on health services, education and so on) is being cut in order that the surplus value thus saved can be diverted into productive (profitable) sectors of industry. At a time when the whole of the capitalist government's policy is geared to restoring the rate of surplus value – by cutting workers' living standards and by diverting surplus value out of 'unproductive' and into 'productive' sectors of the economy – independent cinema is likely to be hard hit.

We can identify two factors contributing to the drain of capital out of the commercial industry. The first is the specific nature of the labour process:

> The process of film production is not very susceptible to the classic modes of capitalist rationalisation (Fordism etc.) and this would be the case with or without the defensive positions which the unions have taken on manning etc. – film production will always be a relatively labour-intensive process. Moreover it is in the nature of the product that it is not subject to that degree of control which makes the capitalist happy. This is true both of the process of production and of consumption; it is difficult for capitalists to 'see' exactly what is happening to 'their' product . . . [These characteristics] combine to make film production appear a risky business from the standpoints of individual capitalists.[2]

The guarantee of massive cinema audiences and enormous box-office returns is enough to offset the banker's nervousness. However, the second factor governing the cinema's decline is the development of the mass entertainment industry as a whole, with overwhelming significance attaching to the advent of television. Since the mid-1950s annual cinema admissions have fallen from over a billion to about one-tenth of that. The present economic structure of distribution and exhibition means that a film has to gross at least seven times its production cost before it is said to 'break even'. As the mass audience dissipates under the impact of television, the inability of capital to control the product, which has been referred to, becomes a critical disincentive for the potential financier. Some films will make a profit; more will not. There is no formula for discriminating, and this is incompatible with the needs of capital.

Some of the proposals in the recent reports on the future of the British film industry[3] attempt to establish artificial mechanisms for the capitalisation of film production which circumvent this obstacle. The British Film Authority will, amongst other things, allow for a restructuring of investment in the industry in such a way that returns to capital accrue over a range of productions. In other words the object is to realise an average rate of profit in order to satisfy the conservative impulse of the bank. However, this will not resolve the basic contradiction of a capitalist cinema. The needs of audiences have changed and are changing. Interest in the cinema is both diverse and particular; there is no longer a single massive potential. There is not, in general, the material basis for individual productions on the scale which capital requires. Ways of producing, distributing and exhibiting films are required which simply do not conform to the processes of 'rationalisation' of monopoly capital. So, 'the cinema is dying'.

The Response of the ACTT

At its annual conference of 1971 the ACTT passed the following motion:

> In view of the total failure of the present privately-owned system of film production, distribution and exhibition not only to provide members of this and allied unions with full employment, security of work and therefore of an assured future for themselves and their

families, but also to ensure the very continuation of film production itself and existence and development of the necessary technical and studio means, this union calls for the nationalisation of film production, distribution and exhibition without compensation and under the control of the elected representatives of the workers in them with a view to serving society properly in its cultural and entertainment needs.

A forum was set up with representatives from all branches of the union to produce a full report to back the demand. *Nationalising the Film Industry*, a 60-page pamphlet published in August 1973, is the product of the forum. In many respects it is an exemplary document. Transcending the politics of trade unionism it establishes the link between the interests of workers in the industry and those of the working class as a whole. In its introduction the document is admirably clear in explaining the necessity of all three terms of the demand 'nationalisation – under workers' control – without compensation':

No act short of public ownership can provide us, the workers in the industry, with a real and continuous exercise of our abilities, and no act short of public ownership can ensure that the community is properly served by the industry.

. . . the experience of past nationalisations has taught us some lessons. It has emphasised the errors to be avoided . . . the scope of past nationalisation has always been insufficient at the outset and the industries, once in public hands, have been manipulated so as to serve the needs of the private sector . . . Basic industries are, in effect, nationalised to assist capitalism rather than to replace it.

We are opposed to compensation for a number of reasons . . . We should not pay for the products of exploitation of the public and workers in the industry . . . The great bulk of compensation would . . . have to be calculated on the basis of current land prices, which are the result of the present criminal property speculation . . . Thirdly, the experience of past nationalisations demonstrates that the financial burden of compensation and interest repayments hinders the crucial early years of the industry's development.

On the whole the report is quite clear that neither the letter nor the spirit of the nationalisation programme can be realised under capitalism. This is most clearly spelled out in an appended paper produced by the union's freelance shop:

> [We do not] aim to see a nationalised industry controlled by trusted appointees of the capitalist state like Lord Robens. We do not want Wardour Street replaced by a bureaucratic machine. When we talk of workers' control, we mean it. When we talk of nationalisation, we mean nationalisation of the basic industries, of the banks and of the land. We mean socialism.

The main body of the paper documents the industry's contraction and empirically demonstrates the inability of the monopoly interests concerned to reverse the process. Its main weakness in these sections is an occasional tendency to moralise and adopt almost chauvinistic postures in relation to capital's 'abandonment' of the industry. However, the history which is produced is one of an industry developed and run down solely for motives of profit by capitalists within the world capitalist economy.

The adoption of the programme by the ACTT and its successful promotion at the TUC, whose official policy it became, represented tremendous achievements for the ACTT membership and for the revolutionaries who fought for it within the union. It has been argued that it is no more than a paper gain but this is the argument of parliamentarians and anarchists. The demand was adopted by the union when the campaign against the Industrial Relations Act was at its height. The programme could lead workers to challenge not only the rationality of capital but also the state itself. In this it breaks through the limitations of trade unionism, which is defined by its defensive subordination to ruling-class policy. The campaign against the Act similarly promised developments within the trade-union movement which would go beyond trade-union limits. It brought millions of rank-and-file workers into direct confrontation with the state, despite the attempts of the TUC bureaucracy to prevent this. The struggle for the nationalisation programme thus occurred in the context of a broad political upsurge in the working class. Developments since then have exposed its contradictory character.

The downturn in class confrontation has created conditions in which the shelving of the demand by the ACTT leadership has passed almost unnoticed. This does not signify the programme's negation.

As it becomes clear that the bourgeoisie has no adequate strategy for rebuilding the industry, the programme will remain as the only coherent solution, from the standpoint of the working class. What remains is the struggle to force the leadership of the ACTT and the TUC to remove the programme from the shelf and lead a serious fight for its implementation.

The Response of the Independent Sector

'Independence' is an ambiguous term. On the one hand it refers to small-scale commercialism – business ventures not directly dominated by monopoly interests. On the other hand it carries political connotations, implying practices whose development is not determined by the constraints of commercialism or by political censorship by the state. Two organisations of film producers, self-designated 'independent', have grown up around either pole of this ambiguity.

The Association of Independent Producers (AIP) represents a 'progressive' section of the bourgeoisie. It is composed of directors, producers and others who have worked in the commercial sector. They seek to establish the conditions for competition with the more successful European cinemas, the French or German 'new waves' constituting models. Their aim is politically modest, consisting of a search for economic formulae whereby untapped British talent can be united with virtuous British capital. They support protectionist and state interventionist reforms as the means of fending off competition from Hollywood and television. Their appeal is primarily to the glamour-starved vanity of a decaying imperialism's intelligentsia who feel a faint sense of shame at the lack of a British art-movie industry. They are fundamentally tied to the capitalist industry as such.

As we have already said, the situation of independent film-makers has much in common with that of workers in the commercial sector in that they face chronic underemployment and under-capitalisation of the means of production. The Independent Film-makers' Association (IFA) is a petit-bourgeois guild seeking to unite film-makers, 'critics' and those involved in small-scale distribution and exhibition.

The film-making practices of IFA members are generally radically different from those established commercially. The differences are partly determined by the comparatively minute scale of the budgets within which these independents are forced to work. At the same time many of the film-makers would defend their working practices as flowing from the particular conceptions of film which they are seeking to develop. Not being directly involved in production for profit, independent film-makers are able to develop a cinema which is not immediately tied to any ideal of popular taste. They can begin to criticise practically the basic structures of dominant cinema from production through distribution and exhibition to criticism. The project for many IFA members is not the production of an 'alternative' cinema, constituting a marginal cultural frill. Rather it is to begin work on a new cinema based on different social relations of production and consumption.

There are very serious problems for those who adopt such perspective. Production in the independent sphere does not take place outside the dominant system of capitalist relations. The subjective placing of themselves outside the industry derives from independents' different methods of work and different relationship to capital – differences which include reduction in the degree of division of labour, flexible crewing standards and different forms of payment. Some of the differences are merely the result of the economic and political weakness of the independent film-maker, while others, such as the departure from industrial forms of division of labour, have a justification in terms of the film-makers' objectives. In defending these specific aspects of their practice, on principled grounds, there is a dangerous tendency for those workers in the union to become identified with the industry in a non-contradictory way. 'Restrictive practices' then come to be seen as the product of the trade union rather than as the response of trade unionists to attacks made on them by employers. In other words class contradictions, which are the real source of the specific practices evolved within the industry, are not recognised as such. Ideally, most independent film-makers recognise the vitally necessary role of the union. In day-to-day practice, however, there is a tendency to regard workers in the union as the upholders of a practice which is antithetical to that of many independent film-makers. This is a petit-bourgeois tendency which in effect identifies the union with capital.

A converse error easily arises out of IFA members' dependence on the state. It appears that the state provides a material buffer between the film-maker and the commercial sphere. The state stands in place of an employer in relation to the film-maker; but the state does not impose the same constraints on the film-maker as does a private employer. The state therefore appears to provide the possible means for developing 'non-capitalist' modes of film production. The converse error, then, consists in a failure to identify the state with capital. Film-makers are pulverised in their relations with the state; fragmented, set against one another in competition for grants, miserably paid and constantly unemployed. Nevertheless, there still exists a tendency amongst film-makers to look to the state for support for a socialist or 'oppositional' cinema. In this way the subjective socialism of a high proportion of IFA members translates itself into an identification not with the workers' movement but with the bourgeois state instead. How does this political displacement occur?

As a section of the petite bourgeoisie, artists and intellectuals experience the capitalist crisis very acutely. The ideology of self-sufficiency is materially undermined. Its contradictory nature is exposed. The petite bourgeoisie is objectively incapable of developing an independent class position on the resolution of the crisis. Ultimately, sections of the petite bourgeoisie are forced to turn for leadership to one or other of the two classes whose historic confrontation determines the outcome of the crisis. However, if the polarisation of these opposing classes has scarcely begun to take a political form, the petite bourgeoisie is slow to learn the lessons of its own impotence. The subjective socialists, while being attracted by the forces of the working class, tend to over-estimate the representativeness of their own experience. Likewise there is an inflation of their social and political role. This expresses itself as political idealism. In the (apparent) absence of a revolutionary leadership within the working-class movement, the revolutionary tasks of the struggle for socialism are understood in substitutionist terms.

An instance of the subordination of political tasks to petit-bourgeois concerns is to be found in the terms of debate offered by bureaucratic and reformist tendencies in relation to the ideological struggle. These tendencies have effectively dispensed with the necessity of socialist revolution as a living theoretical and political tool. They seek justification for this abandonment of Marxist principle in arguments concerning the ideological process. It appears to them that the working class is no longer an actively revolutionary historical force. A process of incorporation, it would seem, has negated its revolutionary potential. This process is theoretically located within ideology. The ideological constitution of consciousness, whereby the working class is subjectively placed in the position of the capitalist class, becomes the object of analysis. The definition of ideology is premissed on the incorporation thesis. The struggle in ideology begins to displace the political struggle for the state, in conformity with the parliamentary perspectives of reformism. Likewise the critique of ideology displaces the critique of the political forms and methods of leadership which are actually responsible for the disarming of the working class. The definition of the ideological process is no longer anchored in the historical contingencies of the economic and political class struggle. Instead ideology is posited in universal and ahistorical terms. Thereby a revision of revolutionary theory, which amounts to its abandonment, is lent theoretical support.

Revolutionary Strategy and the Cinema

In political terms the call for 'struggle in ideology' constitutes an important component of the Communist Party's appeal to petit-bourgeois intellectuals and artists. It capitulates to the petit-bourgeois self-view in overstating the significance of a process in which those layers feel themselves to have a central role to play. In so doing it abandons a clear understanding that the political struggle is decisive in determining the fate of humanity. The significance of the ideological struggle is constantly to be sought in its concrete articulation with the political struggle. Analysis of the former in perpetual abstraction from the latter is academicism.

In the context of the struggle within the film industry, which we have argued must centre on a fight for a leadership which will take up the ACTT nationalisation programme, the petit-bourgeois politics of the 'ideologists' represent an obstacle to the formation of political links between the two sections we have spoken of. Real contradictions exist between the two spheres of production. These are the product of capitalist relations of production. Their resolution is possible only through the successful struggle for socialist relations. The revolutionary left must consequently take care that it does not follow the Communist Party in basing its appeal to film-makers on a revision of Marxism.

Chapter 7

British Film Culture

Claire Johnston

At the present time the cinema as an institution is undergoing a radical redefinition of its institutional space, a redefinition set in motion by the emergence of television as a new form of mass entertainment in the 1950s. In Britain this redefinition, with its new forms of production and marketing to guarantee an adequate return on capital, has led to a situation of instability and 'decline' and to a massive withdrawal of capital from the industry. The studio system has been dismantled and labour has become almost entirely casualised. Production is now largely undertaken by companies set up for one film only and financed through distribution deals; it is in distribution that the real power in the industry is concentrated. The five distribution companies (United Artists, Columbia–Warner, CIC, Fox–Rank and EMI – four of these being wholly on partly American) now exercise effective control over the British cinema and either directly own the dominant cinema chains or control exhibition through agreements.

It is to such a 'crisis' in the British film industry that *The Future of the British Film Industry* (the 1976 Terry Report), *Nationalising the Film Industry* (a 1973 report by the Association of Cinematograph, Television and Allied Technicians [ACTT]) and *The Arts* (a 1975 discussion document for Labour Party policy) are addressed. The Terry Report proposes a reorganisation of the industry in terms of financial rationalisation, making provision for finance by government to encourage private investment. In the guise of nationalist ideology the report proposes effectively a repetition of standard production values – 'films of artistic merit' – and government centralisation. The need for diversification of production and the transformation of distribution and exhibition and the crucial questions of power relations and aesthetics are ignored by the report. The ACTT report, on the other hand, proposes a transformation of the relations of production with nationalisation with workers' control and stresses the dangers of direct state control in an industry handling information, images and ideas. Such a position is reiterated in the Labour Party discussion paper, but the paper also lays an important emphasis, lacking in the other documents, in its proposal that a public corporation be set up to take over distribution, accountable to workers and consumers and free from political interference. It is to this emphasis on the transformation of the relations of consumption that I now want to turn.

Cinema as an institution has an economic and an ideological aspect. Film turns on the production of representations for which people are prepared to pay in order to derive pleasure in a system which guarantees a return on capital. At the present time the cinema as an institution is attempting to discover new forms of production and marketing to achieve this: a redefinition of its space. For Marxists the development of strategic forms of struggle in relation to this redefinition of the space of cinema is now particularly urgent. The move away from a notion of a unified mass market in the industry itself and towards diversification in production and specialised markets (for example, 'soft core' films, 'big screen' movies, the wider definition of 'art cinema') at the same time opens up the possibility of developing an oppositional/'independent' film culture which challenges the ascendency of bourgeois culture. However, the contradictions between what is possible (technological developments, access and so on) and what actually exists is now so great within the institution of cinema that traditional solutions such as unionism have proved insufficient. The emergence of the Independent Film-makers' Movement in recent years, with the aim of developing strategies in relation to both production and consumption through its membership of film-makers, theorists/critics, distributors and exhibitors, could provide a potential basis for such a struggle to displace and undermine cultural hegemony. But the 'crisis' in the film industry itself, producing as it has unemployment and casualisation, has led inevitably to a potentially antagonistic contradiction between unionised sectors of the industry and the political film-maker working in the 'independent' sphere. It is precisely in an analysis of the present conjuncture across the cinematic institution that the terms of the struggle for an oppositional/'independent' film culture can be delineated; such work has barely begun.

Any struggle for a Marxist film culture within the redefinition of the space of cinema as an institution requires a critique of the 'popular culture' debate of the 1950s and 1960s (the work of Hoggart, Thompson, early Williams *et al.*). While the debate can be seen to have served a progressive function at a certain historical moment, its legacy has been to promote a utopian stance among socialist film-makers and critics which has become increasingly limiting within the present conjuncture. As Terry Eagleton has pointed out,[1] such cultural theory is founded fundamentally on the organicist assumptions of Leavis's conservative cultural analysis and on basically social democratic politics. Though progressive in terms of its attack on the traditional assumptions of high art and its exploration of mass entertainment, 'left-Leavisism' nevertheless posed an idealist conception of working-class culture, emphasising its continuities rather than its breaks. Such a monolithic 'positivity' lacks any real sense of contradiction and struggle within working-class consciousness and serves to foreclose any analysis of the ideological determinations (such as labourism and methodism) on working-class culture. As a cultural theory it is unable to provide any analysis of how a strategic struggle against hegemonic culture can be embarked upon. For film-makers, working in the system and outside it, the problem is posed in terms of the control of the means of production and distribution. The whole question of ideological struggle, involving a radically different relationship between production, distribution, exhibition and criticism, is overlooked.

Walter Benjamin pointed out in his classic essay 'The Work of Art in the Age of Mechanical Reproduction'[2] that there is an important difference between supplying a production apparatus and transforming it; it is here that politics become decisive in determining the social space into which the art work is inserted. If we look at the work of Lindsay Anderson (for example, *This Sporting Life*) and Karel Reisz (for example, *Saturday Night and Sunday Morning*) in the 1960s and, more recently, the work of Tony Garnett and Ken Loach (for example, *Kes*) it is possible to discern an uncritical acceptance of the unproblematic nature of the 'popular' audience. For Brecht the notion of 'popular' was a radical concept, embodying an awareness of political strategy. He rejected the notion of the 'masses' as unchanging on the grounds that such an idealist conception was ahistorical and even superstitious, and put forward an aggressive conception of popularity in which people could play a full part in their own historical development through ideological struggle in which the art work is seen as a social practice rather than as an object for consumption. The independent film movement which is emerging is attempting a radical break with such assumptions, but the problem of working out strategies in relation to ideological struggle has yet to be fully worked through.

If we look at developments in film theory over the last fifteen years it is possible to discern a similar break. The popular culture debate played a decisive role in shaping the early development of film theory in this country. The theory of authorship developed by the magazine *Movie* in the early 1960s focused on a reassessment of the Hollywood cinema in terms of its formal and thematic interest, challenging traditional intellectual dismissal of mass entertainment. Implicit in the early elaborations of the theory was the idea that Hollywood cinematic forms could be seen to have a progressive role in terms of British popular culture. Nevertheless, underlying much of this work[3] lay a traditional conception of the art work as an object for consumption, an organic entity. Despite its initial progressive impact, particularly in developing film studies, the early elaboration of the theory captured the American cinema for high art; it failed to provide the knowledge of how a film text functions as an ideological practice. It was Peter Wollen's structuralist reformulation of the theory of authorship in *Signs and Meaning in the Cinema*[4] in 1967 which marked the beginning of a decisive break with such conceptions.

Here film is no longer posed as a communication but as an artefact which is unconsciously structured in a certain way; the author is no longer seen as the creative source but as an effect of the film text. Wollen's book set in motion a series of reverberations through British film culture which for the first time began to take into account recent developments in semiotics and structuralism. This work has been consolidated by the magazine *Screen* since 1971 and further elaborated in terms of theoretical developments in the field of Marxism and psychoanalysis. The importance of this work for developing a Marxist film culture rests in its location of cinema within the relations of production rather than consumption – cinema as a production of meaning involving both film-maker and film-viewer. Cinema is posed as a specific signifying practice which structures and places subjectivity in certain ways. The study of film, therefore, is neither of 'forms' nor 'contents' but of operations, of the process of film and the relations of subjectivity that process constructs; of what kind of 'reader' and 'author' it produces. The examination of cinema as an ideological practice has centred on the analysis of the role of narrative, identification processes, the effect of homogeneity and closure and realist modes within the film text. One of the central effects of dominant modes is precisely the production of pleasure in the viewer through the achievement of an imaginary unity in which closure, coherence and integration dominate, and where contradiction is effectively eliminated. As Stephen Heath has put it:

> The individual is always a subject in society, the point of social and ideological formations, but it is always more than simply the figure of that representation, the excessive turn of such formations. An important – determining – part of ideological systems is then the achievement of a number of machines (institutions) that can move the individual as subject, shifting and placing desire, realigning negativity and contradiction, in a perpetual retotalisation of the imaginary in which the individual–subject is grasped as identity. It is in terms of this double-bind – the statement of social meanings and the holding of the individual to those meanings . . . that the institution of cinema, film as machine, can be understood.[5]

Work within the field of semiotics and psychoanalysis has opened up a way of seeing film as a textual practice and has posed the relationship between the film text and the viewer as the prerequisite for political questions in the cinema as an institution. Film is no longer seen as a form of cultural consumption but as a production of meaning which lays emphasis on the practice of reading films. It is precisely this recognition of the dialectic of making/viewing which forms the cornerstone for developing a social practice of the cinema based on the notion of a struggle in ideology. Such a social practice would see as its aim the breaking of the relations of subjectivity in ideology for the spectator, the setting in motion of a pleasure/knowledge-producing process and the restructuring of desire, through the setting up of a radically different relationship between production, distribution and exhibition.

The importance of the work within film theory for developing a Marxist film culture lies precisely in the way in which representation itself is seen as a political question; the breaking of the imaginary relationship between text and viewer is the first prerequisite of political questions, but it cannot answer political questions or constitute a political goal in itself. The developments in film theory over recent years have had their main impact within the sphere of education and have tended to become academicised and ghettoised to the extent that it is impossible to think and work through a revolutionary practice within film culture at the present time. The 'crisis' in the film industry and the development of the independent film movement have demonstrated the inadequacy of film theory in key respects. Up to now the general assumption has been that the importation of theory is enough to alleviate the deficiencies of film culture; a notion of cultural enlightenment. (In this respect such assumptions exist in Althusser's own work with such concepts as the 'theoretical conjuncture'.) The problem for Marxism has always been how to inter-relate theory with the other practices in the social formation; to consider the political effects of theoretical work. The present ideological barrier between film-makers and film critics, while deeply rooted in bourgeois ideology, can also be seen as a function of the ghettoisation and academicisation of film theory over recent years. The tendency in film theory to divorce the question of the production of meaning from any consideration of the social conditions of production and reception poses an ahistorical conception of the viewer. This forecloses the possibility of working through strategies in relation to ideological struggle in the present conjuncture. Such strategies would involve theoretical work which opens on to the question of ideology as a social instance, involving questions of industry and institutions at particular conjunctures, which examines the relation between reader and text in its historical and institutional specificity.

For a Marxist film culture to exist, film theory and film-making practice need to be conceived in terms of a social practice addressing a particular audience in a particular conjuncture. The redefinition of the space of cinema which is already under way has opened up the possibility for such a social practice to develop. Such a social practice, as Enzensberger suggests in his essay 'Constituents of a Theory of the Media',[6] would involve the location of production in a radically different relationship with distribution and exhibition than exists at the present time in a situation dominated by the laws of the market. Enzensberger's essay is important precisely because it locates the question of the production of meaning in an historical and institutional perspective, stressing the necessity for opening up a radically different institutional space to challenge cultural hegemony. He characterises such an institutional space as essentially decentralised, collective, self-organised; a network system involving interaction, mobilisation and an on-going process of social learning. The social practices of production/distribution/exhibition which have emerged in recent years (for example, the work of the Co-op and political film groups such as Cinema Action) in the area of 'independent' cinema constitute a significant shift in terrain directed towards the opening up of the possibility of a new institutional space for the production of meaning. But, as yet, they have failed to develop a successful strategy in relation to potential audiences. The Independent Film-makers' Movement could provide the impetus for developing this work further both theoretically and practically.

The move away from the notion of a unified mass market within the industry itself and towards diversification renders the development of a Marxist film culture possible for the first time since the 1930s. However, as I indicated at the beginning of this chapter, the economic and the political in relation to the ideological in the social formation have taken on a radically different form which has yet to be analysed. It is only through such an analysis that the effective terms of the struggle for a Marxist film culture can be delineated. At the present time the struggle has focused on the role of state funding and, in particular, the roles of the British Film Institute as a cultural body and the British Film Institute's Production Board. In the light of the Terry Report and the proposed setting up of a centralised state body for film in the British Film Authority, it is important that film-makers and film theorists concerned with the struggle for a Marxist film culture work out an effective strategy in relation to the state which transcends economistic and legalistic interests in order to develop the notion of a social practice which I have outlined. The real danger is that centralisation will lead to the domination of market interests and the work so far developed will be unable to find any effective space within it.

Chapter 8

Their Papers and Ours

Roger Protz

Cecil King, who headed the International Publishing Corporation for many years and who, with Guy Bartholomew, helped remould the *Daily Mirror* in the 1930s, has told of a meeting of the Tory–Labour war-time coalition Cabinet that discussed what might happen at the end of hostilities. They debated whether a situation could arise similar to 1918–19, when an explosion of militant strikes throughout the country put British capitalism under challenge by the working-class movement.

The Cabinet pondered the problem for many hours. Would the returning troops, who remembered vividly the unemployment, poverty and misery of the 1930s, spark an upsurge of working-class discontent? After much soul-searching and head-scratching, they were cheered to hear the opinion of one Cabinet member who suddenly piped up: 'There is a crucial difference between 1918 and 1945 – today we have the *Daily Mirror*.' Whitehall was struck by a gale-force wind as the Cabinet breathed a collective sigh of relief.

It would be absurd to suggest that the relative stability of post-war Britain rested solely on the shoulders of the editorial directors of the *Daily Mirror*, but that unknown Cabinet Minister had, in one pithy sentence, summed up the power of the press to head off the tide of discontent that millions of working people feel under capitalism and to direct that discontent into the safe harbour of reformism.

Effective socialist journalism must be underscored by a clear understanding of the power of the capitalist press. Too many socialists dismiss the mass media as though they were a simple conspiracy to hold down working people. It is a deeper and more complex problem than that. The ruling class has its own philosophy and it is the expression of that philosophy, through the press and television, that confuses and disarms millions of working people. As I write this, an opinion poll shows that an estimated 88 per cent of the population support the Labour Government's latest version of an incomes policy, and once again the power workers have been bullied into calling off a work-to-rule in pursuit of a legitimate wage demand. The terrible isolation of the power workers and the opponents of incomes policy is the direct result of the power of the press to ram home the Government's policy and to pick off small groups that threaten it. It is a frightening power, an iron girder that props up a system long destined for the knacker's yard.

The establishment controls the levers of propaganda. Its members own newspapers right across the class spectrum, from *The Times* on one side to the *Mirror* and the *Sun* on the other. *The Times* is known as a 'respected paper': in other words, it is an obedient voice of the ruling class, described neatly by Trotsky as 'a paper that tells the truth impeccably on every small occasion in order to lie more effectively on the big ones'. It is the internal bulletin of the establishment. The *Mirror*, on the other hand, with a massive readership among working people is a more tangible problem. This paper, as that war-time Cabinet debate showed, is a paper that acts as a safety valve for workers. When capitalism is under pressure it will adopt a radical pose and, through that fake radicalism, will allow workers to give some expression to their pent-up frustrations and anger. Beneath the energetic froth about show-biz nonentities and Royal drones, it is an intensely political paper, far more so than the *Sun*, which, in between the multitudinous breasts, peddles no-nonsense, reactionary tory politics. The *Mirror* is cleverer than that: it knows it is talking to an audience with entrenched anti-tory views and designs its propaganda accordingly.

The *Mirror*'s editions in the run-up to the February 1974 general election were a brilliant example of its ersatz radicalism. It produced some of the most effective anti-tory propaganda ever seen in Britain. Day after day, the *Mirror* ruthlessly pilloried the tories: pictures of chinless public-school wonders were rammed next to shots of overcrowded comprehensives; the mansions of the rich were compared to the slums of the poor; it showed that Britain is a society rent by class and grotesque inequalities of income and opportunity. It helped get out the labour vote and, against all the opinion-poll odds, the Party won the election. But once the election was over the *Mirror* dropped the anti-tory blunderbuss and returned to the more familiar pursuits of undraping ladies and detailing the activities of such socially useful people as the Prince of Wales, with a heavy dose of anti-trade unionism when rank-and-file workers took militant action. The effective role of the *Mirror* is to shackle working people to the established organisations of the labour movement and to the prevailing attitudes of society's rulers.

The socialist movement's propaganda weapons are puny and tiny by comparison. Those with the financial muscle control the means of production and in spite of simpler and cheaper methods of printing in recent years, producing newspapers is still an expensive business, especially without the safety net of advertising. Nevertheless, in spite of all the problems, in spite of harassment and intimidation and censorship, there is an inspiring history of the alternative press in this country stretching back into the early nineteenth century and before. Papers such as the *Black Dwarf*, the *Poor Man's Guardian*, the *Beehive* and the early *Daily Herald* had, for their times, impressive circulations and considerable influence among the radical sections of the working class. Before the advent of the mass-circulation press, the main platforms for ruling-class propaganda in the eighteenth and nineteenth centuries were the Sunday pulpits, when priests would put across the latest line to the faithful. Society is rather more sophisticated today. The establishment has powerful weapons: newspaper sales running into millions of copies a day, backed by television and radio, viewed and listened to by vast audiences.

There is still a frightening belief in the veracity of newspapers, no matter how cheap, vulgar and shoddy those papers might be. Time and time again, when socialists point to some appalling distortion or outright lie in an hysterical tabloid, the stock response is: 'Well, if it's in the papers it must be true'. You don't often hear that kind of attitude expressed about events seen on television or heard on the radio. Television is an instantly forgotten medium, once aptly described as 'moving wallpaper'. The topics of discussion on the bus or in the pub the morning after the previous night's television news tend not to be the news itself but Angela Rippon's hairdo, Reggie

Bosanquet's hairpiece or Peter Woods's 'tiredness'.

Newspapers are still a major influence as opinion-formers and manipulators. They are one of the crucial causes of 'false consciousness' among working people – the adoption of ideas and attitudes that are alien to their own interests. Some years ago there was a strike of steel workers in Port Talbot. They were tough, determined and militant, taking on their own union leaders as well as their employers. They won an important victory and went back to work. A few days later a similar dispute broke out in Scotland and the press asked the Port Talbot men for their opinion of the Scottish dispute. The steel workers condemned the Scottish strikers and said they were 'holding the country to ransom'. That is a sadly typical case of a narrow, parochial outlook; workers can take part in militant action in their own communities and fail to see that their struggles have implications that could be national or even international.

A vital task of the left press is to counter that false consciousness and fight for the supremacy of socialist ideas, not as an abstract ideology but as one fashioned and enriched by workers' struggle and experience. Socialist papers must provide the ideological glue that will join up the disparate struggles of workers. Just like those Port Talbot steel men, groups of workers often fight in total isolation from one another even though their disputes are similar. There are often battles over the same issue, such as the right to belong to and form a trade union, and yet except in the case of a major dispute such as Grunwick, there is no link between workers, no pooling of ideas and experience. Socialist papers can and must provide that framework.

They must point, too, to the contradictions and absurdities of capitalism in order to compare it to a system run under workers' control. This requires painstaking research and investigation but facts and arguments are worth more than a ton of easy slogans. Why are workers on strike? Is it because they are manipulated by sinister reds or are they rebelling against harsh management, vile conditions and low pay? What are the profits of the firm compared to workers' take-home pay? The Marxist concept of the alienation of workers from their labour is often lost as the left press opts for the soft option of sloganeering. On the credit side, however, some socialist journals have widened their scope and their readers' horizons in recent years; most papers are no longer the left's alternative to the *Financial Times*; the class struggle has been fleshed out by going beyond mere industrial reporting to analysing community problems such as housing, education and transport, together with the more immediately political campaigns of the women's and gay rights movements and the crucial need to combat the poison of racism. Important though industrial struggles are, socialism is not just about workers' control of factories; it must be concerned with the whole of society and the quality of life.

Socialist journalism is about providing leadership. Leadership is a tricky word on the left. I do not use it, I hope, in an elitist, manipulative or patronising way; I mean simply that socialist papers must pour themselves into every struggle in an attempt to fuse socialist ideas with the experience of those fighting at the grass roots. One reason why the left today is more isolated that it should be and has not made the gains that it could have made in recent years is that it failed to capitalise on the massive strike wave of the early 1970s and resorted to simple slogans of the 'the-miners-are-fighting-for-all-of-us' variety. But that style of journalism flows from a particular view of the audience for socialist papers. Do you aim for a mass readership or do you concentrate on a smaller audience of more experienced people in the labour movement who demand more than just hand-me-down cliches? It is an important debate, though like so many debates on the left it can be raised to the level of a theological argument more fitted to the Ecumenical Council of the Holy Roman Church than the editorial board of a workers' paper. The dispute at *Socialist Worker* in late 1973 and early 1974, which led to the removal of two journalists and subsequently to the expulsion or resignation of many leading members of the International Socialists, began with an attempt to define the audience for a socialist paper with limited resources and a circulation of about 35,000 copies a week. Some of us felt that the main thrust of the paper had to be towards the more experienced militants. Others argued, equally passionately, that the paper should have a much broader appeal for less experienced and less political sections of workers; they felt that many so-called militants were actually conservative and lacked the potential of younger workers keen to punch fascists and/or soccer referees.

It was a false debate in a sense, because clearly a socialist paper must attempt to reach as many people as possible, often at quite different levels of political development. But until the socialist movement is bigger and stronger, with deep roots in the labour movement, and can afford the luxury of a variety of papers, I remain convinced that the main audience (and I don't like the word 'audience' because it suggests a passivity on the part of the readers) must be the most class-conscious, the most militant, the most experienced, the most political members of the movement – the people with the industrial muscle. But, and it is an important but, the ideas and arguments, the facts and analysis of the left press must reach beyond that admittedly small section of workers to a far wider audience. It was best summed up by an ICI shop steward at Doncaster, who said that most of the material he read in socialist papers taught him little; he was politically experienced and had been in the Communist Party and IS. But he added: 'The way in which you put those ideas across gives me the ammunition that I can pass on to blokes working next to me on the production line and they carry those ideas out of the factory and into their homes, pubs and clubs. You have the ability as revolutionary journalist to put things simply which I can then use to explain issues to my mates.' He was particularly keen to have regular arguments to help him combat racism, which he saw clearly as a crude weapon to split and divide the labour movement.

The left has a grisly ability to create its own splits and divisions. Sectarianism is a deadly disease that kills and maims a healthy socialist movement. It tends to ebb and flow just as the class struggle ebbs and flows and sectarianism, when it is particularly bad, is usually a reflection of the isolation of the left. It is also an expression of the frustration that socialist groups feel at their own inability to grow and extend their influence. Isolation and frustration feed on each other; more time is spent attacking fellow socialists than the real enemy; doctrinal issues become life-and-death struggles to retain ideological purity; socialist papers devote acres of expensive newsprint to denounce the crimes and opportunism of tiny grouplets of deservedly insignificant people; and in the fullness of time a small band of revolutionaries will emerge from the wilderness, purged of all infidels, and announce that *they* – all 500 of them – are *the* revolutionary party. Is it any wonder that thousands of potential recruits to socialism look upon the left groups and their papers with derision and contempt?

Sectarianism has a nasty offshoot. It is a distressing fact that much of the left press is written in a style that is totally alien to its readers or potential readers. Long, drab articles appear to be bad translations from French, Serbo-Croat or Chinese, and Marxism is reduced to a mystical incantation. Too many socialist journalists believe that it is necessary to prove their theoretical virility by lobbing the words 'bourgeois' and 'imperialism' into every sentence. The English language is beautifully simple and expressive and does not need to be hidden beneath a layer of ideological Daddy's Sauce.

If the left and its press are to break out of their isolation, much of it self-imposed, then a major effort must be made to root out sectarianism at every level. Is it not possible for the saner of the socialist groups to stop squandering tens of thousands of pounds in setting up yet more revolutionary print shops? Socialism is about collective action and yet London alone has scores of socialist enterprises pouring out almost identical little tabloid newspapers with red titles incorporating the words 'socialist' or 'worker'.

There have to be differences of strategy and tactics, but such differences are magnified to the point of lunacy. It is time that the left saw sense. There should be one co-operative printing plant where all socialist journalists could unite to produce a newspaper that would be open, polemical and disputative and which could be aimed at a much wider audience than all the groups and papers can hope to reach on their own. It is a paper with the potential to create a situation where working people will say not 'if it's in the papers it must be true' but 'it's in our paper so it is true'.

Chapter 9

Sexism in the Media?

Mandy Merck

A request for a contribution to this collection on sexism in the media presents certain difficulties. The phrase itself has come to suggest a view of the representation of women, indeed of representation in general, now widely debated within the left and the women's movement. To make a virtue of necessity, then, this article takes as its subject a brief review of that debate and an investigation of its implications for feminist analysis.

'Sexism . . .'?

In 1974 the American textbook publishing company, McGraw-Hill, issued 'guidelines for equal treatment of the sexes' to its editorial staff and authors. 'The word sexism', the guidelines state, 'was coined, by analogy to racism, to denote discrimination based on gender. In its original sense, sexism referred to prejudice against the female sex. In a broader sense, the term now indicates any arbitrary stereotyping of males and females on the basis of their gender.'[1]

Similar directions issued by another US publisher, Scott Foresman, put the matter like this: 'Sexism refers to all those attitudes and actions which relegate women to a secondary and inferior status in society. Textbooks are sexist if they omit the actions and achievements of women, if they demean women by using patronizing language or if they show women only in stereotyped roles with less than the full range of human interests, traits and capabilities.'

These definitions, with their use of terms like 'prejudice' and 'stereotype', conformed to similar understandings in this country. Indeed, the American guidelines were models for a draft 'non-sexist code of practice' adopted by a conference of Women in the Communications Industries held in London in 1975: for example, 'There should be no sex stereotyping of abilities, characteristics, interests or activities.'

Such understandings culminated in *Is This Your Life? Images of Women in the Media*, the first book-length investigation of the representation of women in the mass media published in this country. The Introduction reads:

> Our aim is to identify the stereotypes which are still generally accepted in the mass media, and to question whether they are relevant or in the best interests of women. We think we should look closely at how our attitudes are conditioned, and even manipulated, by the media through selection and suggestion. Are the images put out real ones? In what ways are they 'unreal'? And is this due to omission or falsification?[2]

Such a position throws up a host of questions: What would constitute 'reality' in the presentation of women? Are terms like 'conditioning' or 'manipulation' appropriate descriptions of our relation to the mass media? Are the individual media themselves undifferentiated and neutral, functioning only as envelopes around true or false messages? Is the coverage of women's 'achievements' necessarily liberating? Unless we ask such questions, I would argue, feminist intervention within the media are condemned to idealism — lacking analysis either of the materiality of our subordination or of the media operations which contribute to it.

That said, it would be equally idealist to neglect the 'anti-sexist' agitation conducted thus far. The American publishing codes, it should first be noted, were produced under severe legal and financial imperatives. Federally funded American educational bodies are now forbidden by law to purchase teaching or reference materials deemed sexually discriminatory. In Britain, despite the Equal Pay Act and the 1975 Sex Discrimination Act, no such prohibitions exist, although a test case over the 1975 Act's provisions on educational opportunities could conceivably rule several widely used textbooks in breach of the law.

Nonetheless, feminist compaigning in Britain over the last decade has given the concept of sexism (now popularly understood as something like 'the injustice of denigrating the female sex' or 'the injustice of discriminating on sexual grounds') wide currency. And in the absence of previous acknowledgement of systematic female subordination, this has been no bad thing.

A recent article in the International Marxists' paper, *Socialist Challenge,* celebrated this development and noted its effect on the media:

> Scarcely a day goes by when the media does not have some item which — in however distorted a fashion — reveals the growing influence of the women's movement and the ideas it has generated over the past decade . . . In spite of the initial 'outrage' against lesbian mothers, for example, liberal sections of the mass media have sympathetically examined this question. Who could have imagined such a thing even a few years ago? . . . A newspaper such as the *Daily Express* recently published the views of power-workers' wives on why they *supported* their husbands' strike . . . In short, we can now speak of the 'women's issue', and millions of women and men have an inkling of what is implied.[3]

And within the area of media production, it is worth noting recent trade-union initiatives, such as the Association of Cinematograph and Television Technicians' *Patterns of Discrimination* report on the position of women working in the British telecine industries; the foundation of the National Union of Journalists' Equality Working Party in 1975; and a recent amendment of that union's code of conduct to proscribe the origination of 'material which encourages discrimination on grounds of race, colour, creed, *gender* or *sexual orientation*' [italics added].

Yet in the same fortnight that saw the guarded optimism of the *Socialist Challenge* article, the *Observer* asked four leading newspaper cartoonists ('Mac' of the *Daily Mail*, 'Giles' of the *Daily Express*, 'Jak' of the *Evening Standard*, and John Kent of the *Guardian*'s Varoomska strip) for their sketches of women, 1978-style. The results? 'Even in the face of liberation and social revolution cartoonists have stuck to their own dogged and doggish way of depicting women . . . Women on the whole appear as bitching or bitched at.[4]

To what extent (and in which sectors) have the media changed? And why haven't the trade union initiatives produced more in the way of concrete results?

The absence of women workers from key sectors of media production, the embattled position of the media unions in a period of crisis (especially severe in areas like film and newspaper production), and the lack of state intervention (notably the extraordinary inactivity of the Equal Opportunities Commission in the first two years of its operation) all may go some way to explaining why the British media remain largely unchanged in their presentation of women. Another factor may be the largely abstentionist position taken by British feminists towards the media after the antagonistic publicity about Women's Liberation in the early 1970s. Chary of continual sensational or inaccurate coverage, many militants refused to treat with journalists or broadcasters in situations that seemed inevitably beyond their own editorial control. (Nor has the media's presentation of women come under attack recently on the scale of the Miss World demonstrations of the early 1970s, although the national 'reclaim the night' demonstrations against pornography in 1977 and the counter-attacks against the London *Evening News*'s denigration of lesbian mothers in early 1978 suggest an upturn in feminist militancy on such issues.)

But even if these factors were less evident (as they are in the United States) the problem of creating a feminist analysis of the media, and out of that appropriate strategies, remains.

In the United States, the popular feminist magazine *Ms.* sees its strategy as the presentation of 'positive role models'. Issues of *Ms.* regularly feature celebrated American women (in business, politics, the media and so on) whose achievements the reader is encouraged to emulate. Ellen Willis was a contributing editor to the magazine until 1975, when she resigned over its increasing conservatism. In her resignation statement she attacked its

> emphasis on sexual roles rather than male power (changes in roles, in themselves, do not necessarily threaten the structure of male supremacy and may even make it stronger) . . . The common theme is a denial of the need for militant resistance to an oppressive system. We don't need to fight men, only our conditioning. We

don't need to attack the economic system; we too can make it. At best, *Ms.*'s self improvement, individual liberation philosophy is relevant only to an elite; basically it is an updated women's magazine fantasy. Instead of the sexy chick or the perfect home-maker, we now have a new image to live up to: the 'liberated woman'. This fantasy, misrepresented as feminism, misleads some women, convinces others that 'women's lib' has nothing to do with them, and plays into the hands of those who oppose any real change in women's condition.[5]

A similar liberalism can infect the racism/sexism analogy. The original comparison of women's oppression to that of non-whites rightly sought, in the wake of the US civil rights movement and the passage of the British Race Relations Act, to legitimise the feminist cause. And the litmus test insertion of 'women' for 'blacks' exposed an area of public insensitivity which was usefully exploited. But the analogy also tended to despecify the two systems of oppression, to extract them from their particular material relations and group them under the liberal heading of 'prejudice'. Such a separation (for instance, the divorce of racism from any consideration of imperialism) relegates the concepts to the realm of 'wrong ideas' or 'false consciousness' and leaves us no understanding of how or why they should be perpetuated.

Efforts to define a material basis for the relegation of women to 'a secondary and inferior status in society' stimulated two major developments in the women's movement. The first — an investigation of Marx's and Engels's own writings on women's oppression — revealed major lacunae, and even errors, notably in their under-theorisation of the reprodution of labour power, their optimism about the liberating effects of women's entry into waged labour, and their acceptance of the sexual division of labour.

The second development, the practice of 'consciousness-raising', was important in discovering the generality of women's grievances. Women who engaged together in the process of examining 'the stranglehold of one's socialisation into femininity'[6] could no longer view their situation as a strictly personal matter. Consciousness-raising provided a forum for legitimising struggles previously perceived as a matter of the individual woman's success or failure, and the collectively-run small group became a model for the organisation of the movement: 'the rejection . . . of authoritative, hierarchical and competitive ways of relating to other women'.[7]

But consciousness-raising was just that: its target was conscious thought and action, rather than unconscious, and it left a great deal unexplained:

> people felt there was a limit to how much one could get from it after a certain point, i.e. that the construction of one's identity was even more complex and intricately based than had been thought . . . We suspect that the motivation for a reinterest in Freudian theory came as a result of the awareness of how complex the psychological chains that bind us are, and that perhaps it was only subsequent to this that psychoanalytic theory began to be incorporated into a theory of women's oppression in patriarchal societies.[8]

The ensuing rehabilitation of psychoanalysis, once largely rejected by feminists for its ostensible denigration of women, its ahistoricism, and its oppressive clinical application, can be seen as a result of this dual imperative: the desire to extend a materialist analysis into areas unworked by Marx and Engels, and a rejection of the 'conscious' as the sole area of sexual identity and operation. But feminist investigation was not its only point of entry into Marxist theory. The feminist problematic coincided with, and fed into, a new project of Marxist epistemology. This was the rejection of the humanist notion of the alienated subject, proposed as an integral being somehow external to or pre-existing the relations of production, a theory contrary to Marx's fundamental thesis: 'It is not the consciousness of men that determines their being, but on the contrary, their social being determines their consciousness.' The result was a watershed in Marxist philosophy, perhaps best summarised by the French philosopher Julia Kristeva in 1973:

> The theory of meaning now stands at the cross-roads: either it will remain an attempt at formalising meaning systems by increasing sophistication of the logico-problematical tools which enable it to formulate models on the basis of a conception (already rather outdated) of meaning as the act of a transcendental ego, cut off from its body, its unconscious and also its history; or else it will attune itself to the theory of the speaking subject as a divided subject (conscious/unconscious) and go on to attempt to specify the types of operation characteristic of the two sides of this split:

thereby exposing them to those forces extraneous to the logic of the systematic.[9]

A reading of Freud from this perspective, as pioneered by the analyst Jacques Lacan, purported to retrieve his work from its biologism by investigating his assertion that 'the unconscious is structured like a language'. Using linguistic theory to chart 'the subject in process', Lacan examined the coincidence of the castration complex and the child's acquisition of language.

In order that the bisexual infant may take its sexed place in society, an external force (the 'father') must intervene in its narcissistic bond with the mother (the mother wanting the child as 'phallus', the child in turn wanting to be the 'phallus' for the mother). Of course Freud's biological father is in possession of an actual mature penis with which to displace the child and have intercourse with the mother. But Lacan's interpretation of this crisis takes it beyond the biological family.[10]

The intervention which turns the child out of its harmonious identification with the maternal *alter ego* necessarily forces it into the recognition of that with which it cannot identify: difference, lack. Or, as Louis Althusser has written, from

> this dual intercourse in the mode of the imaginary fascination of the ego, being itself *that* other, *any* other, *every* other, all *the others* of primary narcissistic identification, never able to take up the objectifying distance of the third *vis-à-vis* either the other or itself

to

> the order of objectifying language that will finally allow him to say: I, you, he, she or it, that will therefore allow the small child to situate itself as a *human child* in a world of adult thirds.[11]

Within this crisis the 'phallus' is the arbiter, the ultimate signifier of difference, and its possession by the 'father' a guarantee of the social order and the reproduction of dichotomous sexuality in daughter and son. (In boys the separation from the mother is mitigated by the promise of their own latent phallic maturity. Girls, more problematically, are offered only the eventual reception of the phallus in heterosexual intercourse and the subsequent bearing of a substitute phallus, their own child. And thus the cycle begins again . . .)

It is this Law of the Father, then, rather the etymological 'father rule', which informs the Lacanian definition of 'patriarchy': a system of symbolic relations, dominated by the phallus as the arbiter of absence and presence, in which the child learns to mean. In doing so the girl defines her own place within socially-agreed meanings – indeed within symbolising processes themselves – as one of externality and lack.

Stopping here would indeed be ahistorical, since I have sketched patriarchy as a system which so efficiently excludes women as to be virtually invulnerable to sexual opposition. (And feminists have precisely inquired whether such a masculine definition of the cultural order does not exclude, *a priori*, articulated feminist opposition.) But it should be stressed that the marginalising impetus attributed by Lacan to patriarchy does not seek to expel women altogether from the symbolic order (and therefore render them meaning-less), but to delimit them within it. The lack of the phallus, like its possession, is essential to the Oedipal lesson. The system's need to retain the very principle which threatens it is a constant source of instability.

As Kristeva pointed out, the stakes claimed by such a theory are very high: within its terms there is no pre-existing self to be 'conditioned', no authentic womanhood to be misrepresented; nor is there a neutral discourse to turn to feminist advantage. Instead, the power of the 'father', the third term which forever dispels our narcissistic harmony with our mother, is proposed as the basic principle of human meaning, of knowing who we – and others – are, and thus of all our signifying systems. To accept the very constitution of the subject within partriarchal ideology is to raise major questions about feminist struggle and its relation to the signifying practices of the mass media.

' . . . in the Media'?

Those questions might well be first addressed to the cover illustration of the book *Is This Your Life?* Evidently 'this' – an assemblage of cartoon icons headed 'model wife', 'romantic heroine' and so on racked as though for sale – is not; the scowling 'real' woman isn't buying. Inside we find a series of misrepresentation theories applied to various media:

the subliminal effect of this male domination of the air waves [*radio*] should be recognised. It reinforces all the old sexist myths that men are the activists, the speakers, the entertainers – the men who DO – while women are the captive audience, flattered to be chatted up and offered a little second-hand romance along with the idle talk.[12]

The advertiser's misconception about what makes a woman a [*ads*] person, and his lapses into patronizing caricature – by no means confined to Oxo – show how even the most carefully planned advertising campaign can go wrong and why advertising so often enrages women.[13]

So what image have the media, specifically the press, given the liberation movement? Generally it is a reflection of the muddled unflattering and uninformed view that exists in the public mind. A mythical story about a bra being burned in New York grew up some years ago. It never happened, but no woman who dares to suggest that women should have a fairer deal from society has ever been allowed to forget that myth.[14]

One might prefer to have more women DJs; to have Katie spike Philip's Oxo and leave town ('No wild dreams of escape, no hints that she might be bored with serving endless plates of stew', the book laments); to have more press support for feminist struggles. The fact remains that media practices or representations to the contrary cannot be dismissed as myths. Of course contradictions exert their influences, but one could say that advertising, far from misconceiving 'what makes a woman a person', is an important agent in precisely that process.

To insist on verisimilitude in the representation of women leads to grave problems. Recent work on the cinema has particularly noted the tendency of realism to naturalise the *status quo* into inevitability: if this is how 'women really are', how can their oppression ever change? And critiques from realism notoriously focus on the literal, narrative elements in a work, excluding its other ways of producing meaning. Thus in considering popular fiction, *Is This Your Life?* concentrates predictably on plots:

> The typical women's romance story follows a fixed plot, with two possible variations [weak heroine, plucky heroine]. In both versions the poor heroine meets a handsome older man (who turns

out to be rich). He seems to be indifferent to her, or even to despise her. The two are thrown together, on any pretext but love, and, complicated by some promise that can't be broken or some dark secret, the plot gets more and more involved . . . In both versions the thrill of the book lies in the thrill of the chase. Once hero and heroine have revealed their love to one another the book ends. Marriage clearly follows, but there's no hint of what happens after that.[15]

On this basis much of an attack on the Mills and Boon romance could be directed at *Jane Eyre*. Reader, she married Rochester too.

The reduction of a work of fiction to a single structural aspect, in this case its story-line, specifically ignores its 'literariness' – those qualities which differentiate a literary text from any other medium employing narrative, such as film, drama and opera. Nor can such a description formally define the work within literature. (Why shouldn't the quoted account be undertaken in poetry? Would the effect be the same if it was?)

Synoptic descriptions are of very limited use in examining such texts, for it is precisely their combination of a number of structural elements which make them works of fiction. And this combination (for instance, the relation of the narrative commentary to the heroine) vastly mediates the effect of the plot. Thus the story-line cited in *Is This Your Life?* could be presented to celebrate female inferiority; to complain about it but regard it as inevitable; or to indicate essential cracks in the patriarchal edifice which will eventually cause its downfall.[16]

And what if the conventions of linear narrative are wedded to the photographic medium and the result exhibited on a large screen in the privacy of a darkened theatre? Even more predictably, such a specific concatenation of effects goes unexamined in much feminist film criticism. Characteristically, *Is This Your Life?* accepts the conventions of the narrative feature film and questions only the verisimilitude of its heroines:

But all was not lost. The image of women in the cinema, while shrinking, was becoming more realistic. In the sixties, for the first time since the dawn of the cinema, women were allowed to look the same on screen as they looked off it. Elaborate make-up and concrete coiffures simply looked ridiculous in the new realist cinema. Scrubbed faces, flat chests and unarranged hair were the norms for women in such different seminal works as *Blow-up* and *Love Story*.[7]

One could contest this statement empirically (are actresses like Redgrave and McGraw really any less glamorous than their predecessors?) But this sort of objection simply begs the question: is cinema to be compared to a window past which film-makers parade a more or less 'real' life, including its female populace? Is it, in that sense, 'transparent'? Or is cinema itself a signifying practice, a machine for making meanings, including very specific meanings of feminity?

In her recent essay on 'Visual Pleasure and Narrative Cinema', the feminist film-maker Laura Mulvey identified a consistent treatment of the sexes in popular narrative film:

> Traditionally, the woman displayed has functioned on two levels: as erotic object for the characters within the screen story, and as erotic object for the spectator within the auditorium, with a shifting tension between the looks on either side of the screen.[18]

Within the explicit voyeurism of this arrangement, the spectator (whether male or female) is encouraged to identify with the male characters on screen, and to objectify the females. This is accomplished, Mulvey argues, through specifically filmic devices such as the close-up and deep focus:

> conventional close-ups of legs (Dietrich, for instance) or a face (Garbo) integrate into the narrative a different mode of eroticism. One part of a fragmented body destroys the Renaissance space, the illusion of depth demanded by the narrative, it gives flatness, the quality of a cut-out or icon rather than verisimilitude to the screen . . .
>
> In contrast to woman as icon, the active male figure (the ego ideal of the identification process) demands a three-dimensional space corresponding to that of the mirror recognition in which the alienated subject internalised his own representation of this imaginary existence. He is a figure in a landscape . . . Camera technology (as exemplified by deep focus in particular) and camera movements (determined by the action of the protagonist), com-

bined with invisible editing (demanded by realism) all tend to blur the limits of screen space.[19]

As Mulvey demonstrates, this identification of the audience's look at the woman on screen with that of the male protagonist is produced by the special illusion of narrative film:

> This is what makes cinema quite different in its voyeuristic potential from, say, striptease, theatre, shows etc. Going far beyond highlighting a woman's to-be-looked-at-ness, cinema builds the way she is to be looked at into the spectacle itself. Playing on the tension between film as controlling the dimension of time (editing, narrative) and film as controlling the dimension of space (changes in distance, editing), cinematic codes create a gaze, a world, and an object, thereby producing an illusion cut to the measure of desire.[20]

Recasting for less buxom and bouffante actresses, or indeed updating their roles to the aspiring, troubled, semi-independent characterisations of 1970s illusionism (*Klute, Julia*), confirms rather than confronts, the authority of the screen's realism. Such tactics insidiously maintain narrative cinema as the least attributable of signifying practices, a product whose construction is so obscured that the spectator imagines that it emanates from *him-* (the gender is deliberate) -self. His ensuing identification with the hero (and consequent differentiation from the heroine) makes the screen a mirror – a mirror which Mulvey urges film-makers to shatter by reintroducing the intrusive presence of the camera and the audience.

Rather than addressing the cinema as an undifferentiated vehicle of misogynist 'messages', this method of analysis discovers the medium's disposition to produce a particular meaning of feminity. Such an approach (in which film theory is by far the most developed) exposes the false neutrality so often attributed to the varied operations of the mass media. Just as the term 'sexism' is open to critical re-examination, so the blanket designation 'in the media' can now be seen to have encouraged us to regard all media as similar, if not effectively the same.

*   *   *

In 1931 Virginia Woolf's *A Room of One's Own* suggested that a newspaper's treatment of women begins with the design of its front page. The heirarchy of order and headline size, the use of sidebars and feature copy, the differential allocations of space – such devices are not unrelated to the distinction between the grand world of public (masculine) affairs and the lesser one of sexuality, recreation and light relief (feminine).[21] Here, in an excerpt from Woolf's essay, she recalls a lunchtime perusal of such a page after a morning spent reading academic testaments to female inferiority in the British Museum Reading Room:

> Some previous luncher had left the lunch edition of the evening paper on a chair, and, waiting to be served, I began idly reading the headlines. A ribbon of very large letters ran across the page. Somebody had made a big score in South Africa. Lesser ribbons announced that Sir Austen Chamberlain was at Geneva. A meat axe with human hair on it had been found in a cellar. Mr. Justice —— commented in the Divorce Courts upon the Shamelessness of Women. Sprinkled about the paper were other pieces of news. A film actress had been lowered from a peak in California and hung suspended in mid air. The weather was going to be foggy. The most transient visitor to this planet, I thought, who picked up this paper could not fail to be aware, even from this scattered testimony, that England is under the rule of a patriarchy.[22]

A half-century later the scientific apologists for patriarchy are somewhat in abeyance, the National Union of Journalists Equality Working Party has tactfully provided its members with an alternative lexicon[23] ('railworkers' for 'railwaymen', 'synthetic' for 'man-made') – and the front pages of our newspapers look much the same. 'Sexism in the media?' remains an inadequate, and unanswered, question.

Chapter 10

The Mass Media and Racism

John Thackara

The growth of racism during the past few years has been paralleled by a radical shift in the terms of debate on strategies for defeating it. In the early 1970s minority actions by the far left against the National Front were condemned in hysterical terms by commentators and politicians whose line for defeating racists was 'ignore them and they'll go away'. Today, erstwhile moderates vie with each other in denouncing racism and its fascist parasites. The Bishop of Aston announces in blood-curdling terms that if people realised the horror of a developed National Front 'they would lie awake at night sweating with fear'; the Labour Party, authors in government of the anti-immigration policies and legislation that have contributed most to the rise of racism, devote an entire political broadcast to an attack on the National Front; Young Conservatives have even taken to producing anti-racist T-shirts.

A similar change in attitudes has occurred in the mass media. Early in the decade proprietors, editors and journalists would deny the possibility of any link between the media's output and the growth of racism on the streets. But in recent times a number of articles, pamphlets and even the odd book have been written which attack, with varying degrees of ferocity, the role played by the media at least in reinforcing and often in actively promoting racism.

For the media, as for the politicians, this change of heart on racism entails severe problems and contradictions. For leaders of the Labour Party it is becoming difficult to reconcile opposition to racism with a record of vindictive legislation against blacks in particular, and of a pro-capitalist austerity programme in general. The media face a similar predicament, since by beginning to accept some responsibility for the content and effects of their output they begin to explode the notions of balance and impartiality which form the cornerstone of their ideological potency. Anti-racists therefore have an excellent opportunity to home in on these contradictions and transform posturing against racism into effective opposition.

The scope of the problem is immense. Racism operates at every level of society and in consequence permeates most of the mass media's output and structures. Day by day, week by week, broadcasts, editorials and headlines both reflect and reinforce the endemic racism of a society profoundly influenced by its colonial past. This is not to label every media worker a racist – although some undoubtedly are – but to stress that the well-known 'horror stories', such as speeches by Powell or the Malawi Asians saga, are not exceptions but the *extensions* of a series of prejudices and assumptions so deeply rooted that few recognise or question them.

The notion that blacks are, collectively and almost by definition, a problem for society is basic to most media output. Blacks are muggers, scroungers, illegal immigrants, dope-crazed, any variety of misfit and seldom, if ever, parents, children or ordinary members of the community. Blacks above all are portrayed as *different*. Usually reported in a negative context, as an aspect of a supposedly collective problem, blacks seldom get the opportunity to express their own point of view – in other words, racism by omission. Those blacks who do get the chance to speak out can usually be counted on to articulate essentially white middle-class values and aspirations, threatening nobody but saying even less about the true situation of blacks in society. Even blacks who are successful or famous remain black, first of all, when their activities are reported: there are shop-keepers and Asian shop-keepers, teenagers and black youths, immigrants and Rhodesian ex-patriots, sprinters and coloured sprinters.

The episode which shows many facets of the distortion of language, selection of material, sensationalisation and plain incitement was the 'Malawi Asians' story in 1976. It is worth looking at in detail because it was the subject of detailed analysis and scrutiny by journalists as well as by anti-racist groups. The story broke in May 1976 with the arrival in England of a group of tense, wary and frightened refugees. As British passport holders they were allowed entry and temporarily housed in a four-star hotel by West Sussex County Council. The *Sun* broke the story on 4 May with a headline 'Scandal of £600-a-week Immigrants', and was followed by the *Evening Standard* with '£600-a-week Hotel For 13 Asians' and the *Evening News* with 'Storm Over the 4-Star Immigrants'. The rest of the pack followed up with different angles such as 'We Want More Money, say £600-a-week Asians' (*Daily Mail*) and 'Migrants "here just for the welfare handouts"' (*Daily Telegraph*).

In what was a blatant case of racist reporting by most papers in most respects, the 'morning-after' explanations are revealing. The most interesting is a pamphlet[1] by Peter Evans, home affairs correspondent of *The Times*, who identifies four 'notions' whose involvement made the Malawi Asians a 'good story'. These were: first, the belief that 'immigrants live off the state'; second, that the social welfare department is inept and disorganised; third, that 'sponging off the state' undermines the country's fight for economic survival; fourth, that state aid 'saps the vitality of the nation'. According to Evans, the key to understanding how the story built up so much momentum is the concept of 'reverberation': 'for those who do not understand how a newspaper works', he writes, 'there may seem a conspiracy to play up an issue. But news feeds on itself. The utterances of politicians and others help to create a reverberation, with new stories and speeches adding to it in increasingly close succession . . . a mounting clamour that excites the senses and can sometimes drown the still small voice of reason.'

As a description of how newspapers work, this account is interesting. As an explanation, let alone a justification, it totally fails to analyse either the prejudices inherent in the choice and prominence given these 'reverberating stories' or the minute size of the 'voice of reason' in the national media. But the more crucial failure in this account is that it is internal to the media themselves; no account is given of the effects and repercussions of this press campaign away from Fleet Street on the streets of Southall and Blackburn.

The media's harassment of the Malawi Asians was appalling because of the climate it created; the moral integrity of the media was not a central issue. By casting the Sulemans and the Sacranies as scapegoats for the failure of the social services, the media created a climate in which the propaganda of racists baying 'Britain for the British' became both respectable and consistent with the apparently prevailing view. Thus, when the *Sun*, to pick just one example, quoted an anonymous council official saying, 'this is not the first time this has happened, and I can't think it will be the last', it was obvious that 'this' referred to floods of immigrant Asians rather than the failure of the council's housing policy.

By creating a climate of fear and insecurity, the media also set the stage for demagogues to jump in and take the process further. In May 1976, for example, Enoch Powell perpetrated one of his not-so-spontaneous coups by leaking details of the Hawley Report on immigration. This suggested that an apparently infinite number of Asian dependents were awaiting entry into Britain, and afforded Powell an excellent opportunity to warn of 'violence in the streets' and so on. The media's reactions were predictable: 'Immigrant Racket Row' (*Express*); 'Immigrants–How Britain is Deceived' (*Mail*) and 'Powell's Warning' (*Sun*). A couple of days later Gurdip Singh Chaggar was stabbed to death in Southall.

Being outrageous and provocative, Powell makes 'good copy' and knows how to manipulate the press to his own advantage. He is also effective because he baits the media with accusations that they cover up problems, and times his outbursts to receive the maximum publicity. But Powell's greatest 'skill' lies in reading the situation on the streets; his speeches seldom occur during periods of racial quiet. On the contrary they are so timed that his prophecies of violence on the streets often come true. The media hand these successes to Powell on a plate in most cases. By giving Powell prominence as 'big news', by repeating his message in great detail and often uncritically, and above all by *accepting* his premiss that there are 'too many immigrants', the media reinforce Powell's racism by their failure either to recognise that he uses them as a stage or to ensure that his contentious 'proposals' are put in critical context.

While the Enoch Powell press is a national, largely Fleet Street, phenomenon, the relationship between some local newspapers and openly racist or fascist individuals and parties is in some cases more profoundly revealed. The attitude of the *Lancashire Evening Telegraph* to National Party leader Kingsley Read during the latter's trial for offences against the Race Relations Act provides a vivid example of this problem. Shortly after becoming a local councillor in Blackburn, Read was arrested for inciting people not to sell their homes to blacks. The *Telegraph* on 7 May, under a headline 'Jail Threat to Kingsley Read', mentioned the charges only in the seventh paragraph of its story. On subsequent days the paper carried the following headlines: 'I Stand By Jailed House Owner Says Councillor Read'; 'Fighting Fund Launched for Kingsley Read'; '110 Nurses Back Kingsley Read'; 'Read Fund Tops £300 Mark'; 'Party chief's Fund Tops £450'; and 'Kingsley Read Set Free After Pledge'. In story after story the man who said of the murder of Gurdip Chaggar, mentioned earlier, 'One down, One million to go', was afforded extensive free and uncritical publicity. Although probably an extreme example, this case illustrates the tendency of many local papers to identify with racist 'maverick' local politicians; in many cases this sort of relationship occurs in papers which have a monopoly of local coverage and a high proportion of black readers.

The glamorisation or outright support of racists, and particularly of racists who break laws for publicity reasons, helps to nourish the idea that the individuals' views are respectable. By making overt racism respectable, part of the accepted scope for political discussion, the media make respectable the organisations fighting on a racist platform, notably the National Front. This organisation's whole political project is tied up with the need to be portrayed as a 'respectable' party, set apart from the main parties only by the radical nature of its programme. In reality the party is using racism as a means of acquiring and organising political support; the important aspects of its policy–destruction of the trade unions, abolition of democratic rights and drastic administrative repression against *all* minorities–are precisely *not* yet acceptable in respectable politics. By making the organisation respectable, the media prepare the ground for the popularisation of the other policies. But we shall return to this.

It should be apparent from this brief survey of the many different ways racism operates in the media that an *anti*-racist strategy for the media must address not only the content of the media, but the way it is organised and their own relationship with the victims of racism, black people themselves. In our view the key axes of an effective strategy concern employment and the education of journalists themselves; action on media content through the media unions; and organisation outside the media among blacks and anti-racists for greater coverage of black people and their culture, and to deny racists a free platform in the media to expound their views.

There is, on paper at least, almost complete unanimity among proprietors, journalists and the black communities on the need for more black journalists. Journalism in Britain is still a whites-only trade. In the National Union of Journalists, for instance, there are only some forty or fifty black journalists out of a total membership of more than 28,000–slightly more than 0.1 per cent of the entire membership. In the population as a whole, this is a proportional under-representation of 700 to 800 jobs, a factor of 20. Figures for the print unions are not available, a fact which in itself suggests that they do not perceive this as a problem. In broadcasting there are only two or three non-white reporters.

Media managers have a number of pat excuses handy to explain this situation. Their favourite is that 'black applicants don't come forward', which is hardly surprising given the overpowering impression of whiteness prevailing on television screens, front pages and radio programmes. Another popular excuse is that blacks from overseas do not have enough knowledge of English or of British customs to operate effectively. Yet such arguments do not seem to have debarred white commonwealth journalists, many of whom have strange accents and customs, from getting work. But the most common explanation is that blacks are usually 'underqualified' for journalism, a profession with a nineteenth-century craft conscious-ness to rival the most arcane in ship-building or, for that matter, printing. Employers are locked into a social and economic system that relegates all but a handful of black people to low-paid, mainly manual jobs.

It should be obvious, however, that satisfactory coverage of black communities cannot be provided without black journalists. Language problems alone will put white reporters at a disadvantage when working in an Asian area. A survey carried out by the NUJ in Birmingham showed that white journalists often got nationalities and religious so mixed up that an Asian reading a typical article would be left helpless with laughter. This is not to argue that black journalists be sent exclusively to cover black stories, but that they would provide a point of reference in any newsroom which would counteract much of the reflex racism that 'slips in' to so many stories. It is therefore incumbent on journalists and proprietors to operate a policy of positive discrimination in employment so that the cultural, educ-ational, economic and social barriers to black journalists do not remain self-perpetuating.

So long as action on employment remains the province of no

particular section of the media, little progress will be made. Activity within the media on the racist content of so much output has, by comparison, developed considerably in recent times, largely within the NUJ. Historically the NUJ has been incapable of self-criticism concerning editorial performance; indeed, only recently has the NUJ been transformed in practice from a professional association into a trade union. But the impact of the racist 'scare campaigns' in 1976, already outlined, saw the establishment of the Campaign Against Racism in the Media (CARM), a caucus of journalists and representatives of black organisations. The composition of what began as a relatively small group of about sixty ranged from television technicians to local paper reporters, book editors and representatives of various union executives. The basic objective of CARM from the earliest days was to organise broad-based action against those newspapers and broadcasting organisations responsible for the worst excesses at that time. A dual approach was adopted: use of the internal disciplinary procedures of the NUJ; and the application of pressure on the media from outside.

The campaign within the NUJ was focused on the implementation of the union's 'Code of Professional Conduct'. This statute, which members of the NUJ are bound by in rule, is an eleven-point programme covering all aspects of a journalist's work based on an introductory 'A journalist has a duty to maintain the highest professional and ethical standards'. The key clause, however, is Clause 10, which states that a journalist 'shall not originate material which encourages discrimination on grounds of race, colour, creed, gender or sexual orientation'. The code of conduct had been dormant and universally ignored, of course, but with the encouragement of CARM and other NUJ members a number of complaints were laid against Fleet Street journalists who had written articles or drawn cartoons which clearly contravened Clause 10. Although this process was slow-moving and bureaucratic in the extreme, the uproar was immediate. So-called 'senior' journalists seethed with indignation that their professional standards and integrity should be impugned in this way, and much of this resentment found its way into diary columns and other articles. CARM was accused of 'bully-boy tactics' and attempted censorship. For the first time in many years the authors of contentious, racist articles had been challenged by their peers.

The significance of the code of conduct lies in its potential as a control mechanism operated by journalists on their own colleagues; It avoids the problems inherent in attempting to use legislation (such as the Race Relations Act) to influence the media, and it succeeds by promoting the collective responsibility of journalists for their own output. However, precisely because such internal action excludes the people most affected by questionable material (that is, blacks) CARM also began to organise activities which could involve non-journalists.

Taking the form essentially of 'community pressure' on its local papers, CARM initiated activity around two London weeklies, the *Tottenham Herald* and the *Newham Recorder*. Neither was extraordinary for the racism which cropped up in stories, letters and headlines, but both were already controversial for incidents stretching back some months. The North London paper, for instance, which has a large black population in its catchment area, had used headlines like 'Black Girls' Brutal Attack on Home Help' and 'What About Us Whites Asks Angry Councillor'; it had also reproduced without comment an open letter to the Home Secretary from Roy Painter, a leading member of the National Party. CARM approached the local community relations officer suggesting that he call a meeting with the paper's journalists. Half a dozen *Herald* staff reporters subsequently met a variety of local trade unionists, representatives of black groups and other NUJ members. In a sometimes heated discussion, the *Herald* reporters argued that 'a journalist's job is to reflect what is going on in the community'—so if you work in a racist community you get racist news. Confronted with some of the black people in the area who had suffered from racist attacks and discrimination, the one-sided imbalance of this argument was effectively combated, even if the experience was threatening for the journalists concerned. After all, no journalists likes to discover that she or he has been out of touch with the community to such an extent.

In Newham, another area of London where racists and fascists had been active for a considerable period, and where similar circumstances of poverty, unemployment and bad housing had provided them with fertile soil, a similar meeting was organised. On this occasion it transpired that many of the extremely racist headlines attributed to individual reporters, one of whom was present, had been written by sub-editors with the editor's approval. The nature of the problem was different, and the contacts made between the black people present and the reporters laid the basis for greater co-operation in dealing with, in this case, an unsympathetic editor.

The significance of this sort of meeting, others of which took place in areas as widely apart as Bristol and Yorkshire, is that they simultaneously confront journalists with the objects of their stories – and journalists are usually surprisingly cut off from their readers – and that they allow links to be forged between different groups which would not usually have the knowledge or experience necessary to deal with something as intimidating as a newspaper.

The implications of CARM's activity, the breaking down of barriers between reporters and the reported and the application of pressure by the latter and the former, were of great concern to some observers of this development. Jim Rose, for instance, chairman of Penguin Books and a former editorial director of the Westminster Press group of newspapers, spelled out *his* dilemma in an introduction to *Publish and Be Damned!*, Peter Evans's pamphlet: 'Minorities are now part of the fabric of this society', he wrote, 'and prejudiced attacks on them delay their integration and inflict wounds on society itself . . . [but] *this is not to argue for the suppression of news which may bring members of a minority community into disrepute.* This kind of censorship is quite inconsistent with the freedom of the press' (emphasis added). Rose does not deny that the press has often contributed to a climate in which racist violence has been perpetrated on black communities, but he is very concerned that it should be *editors* who determine what is, or is not, published. For him, as for the vast majority of editors and proprietors, 'this kind of censorship by journalists . . . is the thin end of a wedge which could be driven between an editor and his reporting staff'. In other words, any interference in the essentially autocratic powers of the media's managers would constitute an infringement of press freedom because it is in their *own person and judgement* that this 'freedom' is vested.

In practice, opposition to racism in the media does not constitute censorship as most people understand it. The main demands put forward by CARM are 'no media platform for fascists' and 'give a right of reply to blacks and their organisations'. The slogan 'no platform for fascists' has been adopted by a wide range of working-class organisations, and in fact has its roots back in the anti-Moseley campaigns of the 1930s. The lesson of the rise of fascism in the 1930s is that anti-semitism (then) and racism (now) are not ends in themselves for fascists; rather, they are the means by which fascism gains support among a working class divided and demoralised by the effects of protracted economic and social crises. Racism is a threat not simply because of its *ideas*, most of which have been deeply imbedded in British society for generations, but because of its potential for dividing, weakening and eventually destroying the labour movement.

Viewed in this way the supposedly neutral function of the reporter and journalist breaks down: there can be no question of being impartial about racism. Since it feeds on material conditions in society, rather than on some mystical 'unreason', it is simply impossible to defeat racism by argument alone – for example, by balancing a racist article with a 'pro-black' article. However unwittingly done, the publication of racist views in the media can serve only to reinforce existing racist ideas by confirming prejudice and making it respectable.

Unfortunately many journalists think this argument against impartiality constitutes an attack on their professional competence. It is true that our demand for critical reporting of racism goes against deeply embedded ideas, rooted in journalists' training and in the structure of the media. But a lot of hostility stems from a misunderstanding, fostered by many editors and politicians, that 'no platform' for racism entails a news blackout. On the contrary, an essential component of our strategy is continuous *critical* coverage of racism in all its forms. We are asking journalists to be both objective *and* biased, reporting the true facts about the situation of blacks in Britain today, some of which will come as an unpleasant surprise to many people, but also explaining the roots of racism and how the racist parties are exploiting it for their own anti-freedom ends. Furthermore, once more journalists begin to insist that their papers and radio or television shows give blacks the right of reply on the day-to-day issues affecting them, then the necessity for journalists, on their own, to oppose racism in the media will decrease.

By comparison with the summer of 1976, the mass media are probably more sensitive about race coverage today. Newspapers such as the *Daily Mirror* and the *News of the World* have become less reticent in exposing the composition, aims and activities of racist parties like the National front, and many journalists have started to work in their unions, notably the NUJ and the ACTT (television technicians), to establish clear policy guidelines for race coverage which remove responsibility for difficult decisions from individuals on to collective bodies such as union chapels. What is more, the racists themselves are getting more and more rattled by the closing of avenues to free publicity; National Front leader Martin Webster wrote a shrill and hysterical letter to *The Times* when North London NUJ drew up a set of guidelines on race reporting. Even the Press Council, a body never willing to endanger the editorial prerogatives of proprietors and editors, has conceded to journalists the right 'in conscience' not to work on racist copy.

The acid test, however, will come at future general elections, where the National Front, by standing hundreds of candidates, will likely be entitled to peak-time party political broadcasts. As a platform for racist propaganda, such an event would put a hundred newspaper articles in the shade. What is more, when it comes to control of the airwaves, the prospect of interference by anti-racist bodies is likely to generate a hostile reaction from the broadcasting authorities. However, a number of MPs and labour-movement bodies (such as the ACTT) have signed an open letter demanding that the National Front be given no access to television facilities at the next election. The ACTT also adopted a code of conduct, similar to the NUJ's, late in 1977. The recent agreement between the NUJ and the NGA, pledging union support to any members whose consciences will not allow them to handle racist material, is another important sign of growing anti-racist resistance. Such a policy will, of course, have to be implemented by rank-and file workers themselves if it is to prove effective. Nevertheless, the terms of the debate on racism have changed irrevocably, and the motto 'If you're not part of the solution, you're part of the problem' is acquiring greater meaning both within and without the media.

Chapter 11

'Press Freedom': a Socialist Strategy

Geoffrey Sheridan and Carl Gardner

The first condition of freedom of the press is that it is not a business
activity
Karl Marx

It is not the main intention of this article to *convince* the reader that
we do not have a 'free press'[1] in Britain. The starting point of our
argument is that the mass media in general are owned and/or
controlled by a minute, unelected section of the population. In turn,
they are almost totally run in the economic and ideological interests
of a fractionally larger, similarly unelected minority, the owners of
capital – what has been classically termed the 'ruling class'. The
proprietors and managers of the large majority of these media are
indeed part of that same ruling class. It is our contention that such
ownership and control has led to systematic misrepresentation in the
reporting of the lives and activities of the large majority of the
population, including several significant, oppressed minorities. This
is the result of a process of exclusion or distortion of a wide range of
views from the mass media, and the presentation of a general
'consensus' world-view which corresponds with the needs of capitalism to maintain its hegemony. We should add that, except in the
minority of cases, there is no implication of a vast, conscious
'conspiracy' here. In the view of most trustees, proprietors, editors

and journalists, what is presented in the media is sincerely seen as 'objective', natural truth – hence the smug righteousness which surrounds their claim to be *the* upholders of a 'free press'.

We start, then, from the contention that we do not have 'press freedom' in Britain, despite the protestations of countless leader columns to the contrary. We are not alone in this contention. After all, even that not-so-revolutionary body, the TUC General Council, in its submission to the Royal Commission on the Press, stated: 'The fact that eight men control 90% of Britain's papers means that the concept of "freedom of expression or independence of editorial" is somewhat Orwellian.' Nevertheless, for those not convinced of this premiss, we shall be adducing some facts and examples to support our case. We also recommend various studies which have been recently published. These are not related simply to the economic owner-ship/control of the mass media, but critically cover the effects of ruling-class domination of the principal sources of public infor-mation: recent media coverage of trade-union affairs, women's and black activities, and the war in the north of Ireland.

Most of our attention will be concentrated on outlining briefly the assumptions that lie behind the 'press freedom' arguments and the way that these assumptions have been used to ward off threats to the present monopoly. Secondly, we will give a brief account of the effects of reporting, mentioned above. Thirdly, we shall look critically at the various strategies for changing the present situation, put forward by sections of the labour movement and the left. Lastly, we will be advancing the outlines of what we consider to be a revolutionary socialist strategy for the media, which both begins to tackle effectively the problems confronting us today and can lead to the establishment of a genuinely free press within the context of a socialist society. Such liberated forms of media must answer the needs of and involve and represent the vast majority of the population – a condition which we take to be the *sine qua non* of genuine press freedom.

This is precisely what the present forms of media do not do, and the reasons are not difficult to find. The actual figures to which the TUC General Council referred are the following: six companies – Reed International, News International, Trafalgar House (formerly Beaverbrook), Associated Newspapers, Thomson and Pearson Longman (which in addition to the *Financial Times* owns the provincial chain, Westminster Press) – publish 80 per cent of *all* daily and Sunday newspapers in Britain. There's a new definition of 'freedom' for you! Or rather, an old one given new life.

But the extent of monopoly control does not end there. A growing feature of late capitalism in Britain has been the penetration of newspaper capital into other sections of the media, especially radio and television – quite apart from such other interests as property and oil. In addition one can see this process working in reverse, with the increasing take-over of the press by other sections of industrial and finance capital. The property consortium Trafalgar House recently bought out Beaverbrook, and the multi-national oil concern Atlantic Richfield gallantly stepped in to 'rescue' the *Observer*.

So, too, six of the 'independent' (independent from whom?) regional television stations are owned substantially by one or other of the newspaper giants. The most prominent is News International, which is the largest shareholder in London Weekend Television; Associated Newspapers owns 37.5 per cent of Southern TV; and Thomson Newspapers has a 25 per cent stake in Scottish TV. Similarly several 'independent' radio stations are partly owned by the same tightly-knit group of press concerns – News International, Associated Press, Trafalgar House, Thomson and Reed all own substantial shares in local radio.

In addition, as Raymond Williams points out in his opening contribution to this volume, one peculiar feature of the press in Britain, compared with that of other European countries, is the extraordinary degree of dependence on advertising revenue – for example, without advertising, the *Financial Times*'s cover-price would be five times higher than it is now and the *Daily Mirror*'s three times higher (1975 figures). This has had, and continues to have, two inter-related effects. First, as Williams points out, many newspapers with very respectable circulations – often towards the left of the political spectrum – have had to close because of lack of advertising revenue. The *News Chronicle* and the *Daily Herald* are just the most recent and lamented examples. Secondly, the effect on the remaining papers is a concentration of advertising and an increase in the implicit influence of advertisers to maintain a particular editorial policy.

The most publicised example of how this works in its extreme form was shown in the case of the *Guardian* (then the *Manchester Guardian*) in 1956. The *Guardian* was the only mass British daily to oppose Eden's imperialist adventure in Suez. Advertisers withdrew over a third of current advertising immediately, and if it had not been for the subsidy from the profitable *Manchester Evening News* and unusual support from the paper's trustees, the editor would have undoubtedly been sacked or forced to change his line. After all, the *Guardian* had built its credibility on firmly-held, liberal values, which had to be *seen* to be upheld. Other newspapers in Fleet Street have not even got those rather wobbly crutches on which to lean. On a wider scale, the implications are not difficult to see.

So this strong proprietorial monopoly, interwoven with both subtle and crude financial pressure on the part of advertisers, rather emphatically undermines the whole pretence of 'press freedom'. What 'press freedom' means to a Thomson or a Murdoch is the freedom to appoint the person of his choice, to decide autocratically what shall and shall not reach the eyes of millions of readers. In turn his (and it is invariably *his*) subordinates understand the general limits within which to report, and trim their copy accordingly. Much of this is unspoken – many journalists share their editor's social and political assumptions. But in any case there is not a lot of 'freedom' involved in such a process. *En route* the paper is expected to make money, generally by satisfying the capitalist advertiser. At present both goals are in principle satisfied at a national level by a conservative editorial policy: six of the eight major Fleet Street dailies more or less support the Conservative Party; one – the *Daily Mirror* – supports Labour; and one – the *Guardian* – is never quite sure. Not a lot of 'freedom' there, either, at least in terms of political expression. The political spectrum represented – from centre labour to right-wing tory – is probably the narrowest of *any* national press in western Europe.

But we must be cautious about regarding the media simply in economic profit–loss terms. Admittedly the current attempts to get new technology installed in Fleet Street are aimed at reducing jobs (variable capital) and thereby raising the rate of exploitation and productivity – such is the operation of capitalist investment anywhere. However, the importance of the press for the proprietors and the bourgeoisie as a whole is much more located in ideological/political terms. Beaverbrook never made any secret of why he owned newspapers – it was minds, not money, he was after. So too Roy Thomson was willing to run *The Times* at a loss for many years – that can't be explained by a mere economic interpretation. Enzensberger, in his lesser-known essay 'Industrialisation of the Mind', has this to say:

The products of the mind industry can no longer be understood in terms of a sellers' and buyers' market, or in terms of production costs: they are, as it were, priceless . . . to concentrate on their commercialisation is to miss the point and overlook the specific service which the mind industry performs for modern societies . . . The mind industry's main business and concern is not to sell its product: it is to 'sell' the existing order, to perpetuate the prevailing pattern of man's domination by man, no matter who runs the society, and by what means . . . an entire industry is engaged in . . . eliminating possible futures and reinforcing the present pattern of domination.[2]

Now Enzensberger was talking principally about electronic media, especially television and radio (where obviously the direct commodity-relationship is considerably reduced). But such an approach is an important key to understanding the functioning of the British press and the ritual song-and-dance before the altar of 'press freedom', so solemnly and regularly enacted. It would be a reasonable hypothesis to warrant that one aim of the general outward diversification of newspaper capital into the radio/television/leisure fields, as well as others, is precisely to enable those proprietors to 'subsidise' their newspapers – a buffer against closure. Beaverbrook was in such trouble recently over the *Evening Standard* because it is one of the few newspaper companies which has not diversified significantly in this way. Such ideological/political organs are worth far more for the maintenance of the system as a whole than mere money in the bank. In other words, the media are as much involved in the reproduction of the relations of production in general as in the individual accumulation of surplus-value. Those socialists who try to reduce every action of the press proprietor to the rapacious attempt to accumulate more and more *individual* wealth, in the form of profits, will understand only part – and the more obvious part – of the operation of that particular sector. This was particularly evident around the journalists' closed-shop issue, as we shall see.

Let us, then, examine the 'press-freedom' ritual and the way that it is constantly able to renew itself, despite all the evidence to the contrary. The first presupposition which underlies all discussion of this issue is that the British press is not just 'free', but the *freest* imaginable. Certainly in comparison with South Africa or the Soviet Union, the ideologues of Fleet Street can claim a relative degree of diversity of opinion. But the content of the press in Britain is not simply a function of the liberalism and honesty of editors – it is a function of the overall balance of class forces which surround those media, ensuring a limited responsiveness to different currents within society. Such is one of the historic gains of the bourgeois–democratic stage of social development, which must be preserved and *extended* and for which the strength of the workers' movement *alone* can be relied on.

Flowing from this is the constantly reiterated myth that those who challenge the present proprietors' monopoly wish themselves to establish a press based on the Soviet model. This is simply a convenient lie. For the proprietors and the bulk of press commentators, supported unquestioningly by the main political parties and government, 'press freedom' = private ownership and the running of the media according to commercial criteria (that is, market forces). This is coupled with the fig-leaf of the 'independent' BBC plus such toothless watchdog committees as the Press Council. Three Royal Commissions on the Press since 1945 have noted the 'shortcomings' of this set-up – but inevitably almost nothing has been done to change it.

The other assumption is that 'press freedom' is best preserved by leaving the reporting of news to journalists and editors. Such specialists, it is argued, have special powers acquired through training and experience which enable them to remain 'detached' and to report matters more truthfully and 'objectively' than others. Somehow they are able to take a 'neutral', 'detached' stance, free from the prejudices and influences of mere mortals. In particular, the role of the editor has become one of an ultra-privileged superperson, whose freedom is unchallengeable. This is the mystique of journalism which we, as socialists, must reject as dangerously elitist, a central prop for parliamentary democracy, and totally misleading in its conception.

The first assumption of our strategy is that the media are too important to be left to journalists alone. As we have seen, the press has never been free from direct or indirect influence by capital. We favour an enormous extension of influence, towards the involvement and access of the mass of the working population and of minorities and their organisations, to every branch of the media. In addition we reject the whole concept of 'neutrality', 'detachment', 'balance' and the rest of such terminology which is meaningless when applied to the mass media except as a justification for the *status quo*. All expressions of opinion, explanations, ideas and interpretations of facts – in short, all communicable knowledge – has a social function and satisfies some need or purpose of an individual or group character. All writing serves some social end – there is no such thing as neutral reporting, despite the fondly protected self-image which many journalists nurture. Journalists do not just report the world 'as it is', like passive recorders – they, and the editor who decides *which* incidents they should cover in the first place, select, colour and interpret, according to their own needs, experience, views and purposes, and those of their newspapers. These needs often reflect and coincide with larger group or class interests. How, for example, could the capitalist press ever be consistently objective about the ideas or activities of trade unions? They have no interest in doing so – proprietors and editors have social purposes and aims totally opposed to those of the trade union movement. The extensive tendency towards 'self-censorship' which Andrew Goodman has described in detail in relation to the BBC[3] is part and parcel of this process.

Now, as socialists we do not think that this is to be regretted. It surely makes public debate and discussion much more comprehensible if everyone declares in advance her or his own 'purpose' – their aims, interests and identifications. We have done precisely that in this essay. What is objectionable is where class or group interests are daily hidden and disguised under the spurious garb of 'impartiality', as in our national and local press, or where class interests are disguised under the dishonest rubric of the 'national interest'. Similarly, what doubly obscures is the pretension of some group (or individual) to be the privileged holder of some greater, more truthful 'truth' than others – this is precisely the role that editors, supported by the capitalist establishment, claim for themselves. And it is this role that the working class must challenge as an essential part of the struggle for a freer press and a freer society.

The situations which have aroused the most heat on this issue, at least on the part of the editors and proprietors, have been those rare cases where the workers on a particular newspaper – printers or journalists – have intervened because they strongly disagreed with the ideas expressed in that paper. Most of these cases, which are detailed in John Whale's book,[4] have revolved around reporting of trade-union affairs. Such moves on the part of the print unions have a long, if somewhat interrupted, history – after all, it was the refusal of the *Daily Mail* workers to print a lead article entitled 'For King and

Country' in 1926 which gave the government an excuse to break off talks with the TUC, and thus precipitate the General Strike. One more recent example, which was excellently handled by the print workers, was the stoppage at the *Observer* on 25 and 26 June 1977. They objected to a display advertisement put in by the National Association for Freedom calling for financial support for the Grunwick management against the trade union movement's attempts to get APEX recognised there. They demanded the right of reply on behalf of the print chapels at the *Observer* in solidarity with the Grunwick strikers and eventually, after some hours, got a front-page statement in the late editions. This action was endorsed by the executive of the National Graphical Association – the first occasion in recent history where a print union has officially sanctioned intervention by its members on an editorial issue. In some other disputes print chapels have simply obstructed production, giving credence to management accusations of 'censorship'. However, the demand for the 'right of reply', by or on behalf of the injured party, alongside the original, offending article can carry no such stigma and is, as we shall argue, one of the keys to the door of a genuinely free press. Of course managements may refuse such a right – in which case it can be clearly seen to be they, and not the workers, who wish to limit diversity of opinion in the press. This was certainly the case, for example, when the editor of the *Financial Times* included details of printers' pay but refused to include details of journalists' in the paper's report of the first findings of the latest Royal Commission on the Press.

The other issue which has caused the most discomfort among the upholders of 'press freedom' has been recent government legislation permitting the NUJ to set up the closed shop. This will be examined later, particularly in relation to the inadequate response of the NUJ to the employers' anti-closed-shop campaign.

One result of the media's implicit purpose – to sell the existing order (that is, capitalism) – coupled with the journalist's belief in herself or himself as 'objective' scribe of things-as-they-are is that large sections of the population are grossly under-represented or misrepresented in the media. In addition, particular issues of a sensitive nature are distorted or omitted. These effects are the inevitable result of the editors' and journalists' conscious and unconscious collusion in maintaining the (capitalist) *status quo*. In response, it is the duty of those groups and individuals who suffer as the objects of such 'dispassionate' reporting to form the counter-weight which can begin to challenge that misrepresentation, resist the spurious arguments of 'censorship' and gain increasing access for themselves and others in the press to put their views.

At present the forces which can play such an initial role are to be found in the women's movement and among blacks and trade unionists. In addition, all these forces, and the left in general, should be prepared to take a stand against the almost total media censorship and distortion of the imperialist war in the north of Ireland. Jonathan Dimbleby's revelations in the BBC programme *What do you think of it so far . . . ?* in August 1976, and in Newsreel Collective's film *Before Hindsight,* and the setting up of a 'Free Speech on Ireland' campaign, are welcome first steps on this front.

We do not have space to cover the way that these various groups – women, blacks and trade unionists – get a raw deal in the media. We would refer readers to the two essays in this volume on the questions of racism and sexism in the mass media and to the bibliography, plus the various detailed studies which have been done on coverage of trade union affairs. All of these show distortion, misrepresentation and omission of a quite pronounced character. None of these studies has been adequately answered, except by a libel writ by ITN against the Glasgow University Media Group for their book *Bad News*[5] and general vilification of the authors as 'enemies of press freedom' in the case of the Campaign Against Racism in the Media's pamphlet.[6]

We regard this evidence as fairly conclusive. Indeed, in the light of such evidence, we are tempted to ask which sections of the population have ever been treated fairly in the British press – English, white, male stockbrokers, perhaps? But, more importantly, what can be done to turn the tide, to change this miserable state of affairs? Some solutions have already been offered, by various sections of the labour movement and the left. It might be useful to examine these briefly, to spotlight their deficiencies.

One proposal was researched and put forward by the National Association of Local Government Officers (NALGO) at the 1976 TUC. Here they proposed a TUC-funded monitoring/research unit to look at media coverage of trade union affairs in a rigorous manner, so that complaints about bias could be more accurately drawn up and argued for. The cost of this scheme was assessed at about £100,000 per year – or roughly 1p per trade unionist. Although such a scheme would be a valuable adjunct to the struggle for a free press – provided that the findings were accessible to the *whole* movement – such a proposal does not *in itself* begin to challenge the existing pattern of ownership/control of the media.

Various sections of the movement have put forward proposals for new 'watchdog' committees, over and above the perennial proposal to 'strengthen' the Press Council. These have included such bodies as a Public Broadcasting Commission (suggested in 1974 in the Labour Party document *The People and the Media*), a Public Committee for Broadcasting (the Annan Committee report, 1977), a Ministry of Communications (Labour Party document on *The Arts*, 1975) and a Broadcasting and TV Council (Raymond Williams, in *Communications*, in 1966). There is no space here to discuss the minute ramifications of these various schemes.[7] Nevertheless, it is possible to point to several weaknesses in all these proposals. Firstly, there is the obvious fact that some are limited to broadcasting, while others (*The Arts*, for example) are totally ambiguous as to whether the press should be included. It is our contention that the whole media must be taken together, particularly given the considerable interpenetration of the various media capitals in recent years. The problems of freedom and access are essentially the same in all media forms. But the principal problem with these schemes is that they rely for their implementation on either sections of the capitalist state apparatus or the trade union and Labour Party bureaucracies – all of which, for different reasons, are not renowned for their tendencies to carry out radical change. In the case of the former, the capitalist state's principal function is to defend capitalist property relations in general and the rule of private capital as a whole. Yet the problem of the media is precisely the virtual monopoly of private ownership/control by individual capitalists or groups of capitalists. None of the formulations offered is prepared to recognise this fact, or its corollary that the most effective solutions to the problem of the media and democracy can only be resolved by direct, mass action and involvement by those presently excluded: in other words, the majority of those working in and being reported (or not reported) by the media. We must strongly oppose all those who would hive off discussion and implementation of media policies into government commissions or similar bodies.

One strategy which has been advanced to deal with this problem (and one which neatly sidesteps it) is the proposal to set up a mass daily labour-movement paper, which the working class has lacked since the demise of the *Daily Herald* (part-owned by the TUC until 1961) in 1964. This is particularly close to the heart of Bill Keys, general secretary of the print union SOGAT. Such a step would be positive step forward for the British labour movement in terms of re-establishing and extending its own independence on the terrain of mass propaganda. The loss of the *Daily Herald* – despite its middle-of-the-road social democratic policies – was a genuinely-felt one. However, there are certain problems with this proposal, not the least of which is simply financial. Estimates given for the scheme are as high as £7 million even to set it up. But the bigger problem is political – such a paper, controlled as it would be by the labour bureaucracy, would undoubtedly reflect the politics of those bureaucracies, as well as a whole series of conservative assumptions concerning style, form and presentation. Such an editorial policy would in general not be guaranteed to ensure massive sales. In addition, there is no evidence, from a perusal of the large majority of trade union journals, that they are any more democratically run than the denizens of Fleet Street. They are in general mouthpieces for the trade union leaders, pure and simple. Little democratic debate and exchange of ideas by opposed currents and political formations in these unions is permitted. Such debate is vital for an interesting and *useful* workers' publication. The NUJ's journal is one of the few exceptions – the editor of the *Journalist* is subject to re-election every three years by the membership, and is not appointed from above. Lively, untrammelled debate takes place in its pages and the paper is permitted to report in detail the discussions which take place on the NUJ's Executive. This was the result of the successful fight put up by its first elected editor. The general lack of democracy within trade union journals must put our trade union leaderships in something of a quandary when it comes to arguing for more 'democracy' and access in the national press – which probably explains in part why it has never been one of their major priorities. In spite of all these inadequacies, it has to be emphasised that socialists need to support *any* move to gain the workers' movement greater access to the mass media or an extension of its own limited media resources.

More radical proposals have been offered which bear con-sideration. In a supplement on 'Press Freedom' in the *Journalist* of January 1975 there appeared an article which proposed a national public printing corporation, to which interest-groups would apply for resources and time to print their journals. The TUC, NUJ,

NATSOPA and NALGO have all put forward more modest variants of this at different times, though in their proposals such a corporation was generally conceived of as existing *alongside* rather than *in place of* the present press and publishing companies. The scheme outlined here goes beyond that and formally and administratively corresponds to the kind of scheme which Lenin envisaged and advocated in the early years after the Russian Revolution. However, in the present situation the problem cannot be solved merely administratively, or by propagandising for an ideal scheme. Firstly, nowhere does the *Journalist* article specify the *nature of the state* which would be willing or able to implement such a scheme. It is unlikely that such a scheme would be possible under capitalism. A precondition for such a system would be the establishment of a workers' state and the expropriation of private capital, plus a large degree of state planning. But even if it were possible under capitalism, there are no proposals relating to the kind of struggles necessary to establish it. Such proposals in no way link with the present level of struggle and the tendencies within the media today. In the absence of such a set of tactics, embodied within a general strategy, the only interpretation of these proposals which can be understood is of a bureaucratic process of imposition from the top.

What, then, are the elements of such a strategy? For a start, socialists have to be in forefront of the struggle for the extension of media access and greater 'press freedom'. Central to this at the present time is the demand for the right of reply in the press and on radio and television. Wherever there is an instance of distortion or misrepresentation in the media, the right of reply of equal length for the individual or group involved must be demanded. For example, why should Bernard Levin be able to intervene, to the tune of regular 1500-word contributions, in the union elections in the AUEW (1976) or the NUJ (1977) in favour of the right-wing candidates without the left being given equal space to reply? All attempts simply to *exclude* views must be energetically opposed – even the reactionary babblings of a Bernard Levin or a Peregrine Worsthorne. Print workers and journalists must be encouraged to secure the right of reply, first and foremost.

The only exception to this principle is the case of the fascists – at present principally the National Front. We are not in favour of the media being given over to those whose speeches lead to attacks on and murder of black people up and down the country. Surely even liberals do not claim that, if Hitler came back to stand in an election, he should be given equal press and air time with other politicians. Or that someone who advocated dangerous driving, in unsafe cars, would be given media-time to expound their lethal views. For us, the fascists are much more dangerous creatures.[8]

The NUJ code of conduct, binding on all members of the union, includes the following clauses:

2. A journalist shall at all times defend the principle of the freedom of the Press and other media in relation to the collection of information and the expression of comment and criticism. He/she shall strive to eliminate distortion, news suppression and censorship.

3. A journalist shall strive to ensure that the information he/she disseminates is fair and accurate, avoid the expression of comment and conjecture as established fact and falsification by distortion, selection or misrepresentation.

4. A journalist shall rectify promptly any harmful inaccuracies, ensure that corrections and apologies receive due prominence and *afford the right of reply to persons criticised* when the issue is of sufficient importance.[9] [Emphasis added]

The code of conduct of the NUJ should be used, both by those inside the NUJ and by those outside. It should be popularised in the wider labour movement, particularly Clause 4 and Clause 10, which forbids the origination of material 'which encourages discrimination on grounds of race, colour, creed, gender or sexual orientation'. Journalists must fight for the right of reply for those they feel have been misrepresented. Trade unionists, women, gays or blacks should approach offending NUJ members or chapels to demand its implementation. Members of the NUJ not upholding the code of conduct can be disciplined by the union.

This is a start. The essential aspect of any effective strategy is that it must put the question of *press content* at the centre of every issue involving the media, for that is the terrain which the editors and proprietors hold sacred and, like Samson's hair, where their strength lies. This applies equally to those outside the media and to those inside. Working on the principle that the media are too important to be left to journalists alone, contacts and links must be forged between journalists, print workers and the broader movement outside over this issue. If journalists are unresponsive, pressure must be applied by labour movement bodies, and others, in the form of pickets and demonstrations to get a change of policy. Such tactics can be especially effective on local papers and radio stations, which are much more susceptible to local feeling, though direct action of this kind against Fleet Street papers and the national broadcasting companies can also bring results. An excellent example occurred in January 1978 in response to a sensational, witch-hunting (and dishonestly obtained – the strapline was 'How I Posed as a Lesbian Mother') story in the London *Evening News* against lesbians being permitted artificial insemination (AID) in order that they could bear children. The day after the story's publication, over twenty feminists, socialists and lesbians occupied the offices of the *Evening News* and collectively confronted the editor, despite physical harassment and a barrage of abuse from members of the *News*'s staff. Their action forced the editor to concede a detailed 'right of reply' in the following Tuesday's edition, defending the right of lesbians to bear children and rejecting the *News*'s self-created 'right' to judge their suitability for maternity. Such initiatives will, it is hoped, be imitated elsewhere.

For journalists, the whole question of an alliance with the broader labour movement, including the printers or broadcasting technicians, is vital. The reputation of journalists among the broad labour movement is pretty low, for obvious reasons. They are seen as the people who originate anti-trade union, racist or sexist copy on a routine, day-to-day basis. Often it is not necessarily that individual journalists are anti-trade union, racist or sexist, but that they see their job, wrongly, as being to simply 'reflect' or 'record' society as it is. This obviously includes such ideologies in quantity. While many journalists do unfortunately hold such views themselves, an increasing number – particularly in the local and provincial press – are beginning to challenge the editors' claims to be the trustees and sole executors of press freedom. This is increasingly the case on issues of race and anti-trade unionism. Given the relatively isolated and weak position of the NUJ, such moves are vital steps in building the support and solidarity in the rest of the working class, particularly the print unions. This would greatly strengthen the NUJ's position, even on the bread-and-butter trade union struggles for better pay or against redundancy.

The whole problem can be best seen in considering the recent struggles around the post-entry closed shop in the NUJ. During the tory administration of 1970–4, the closed shop in industry had been outlawed. The Labour Party on returning to power in 1974, was committed to reinstating it. This, Michael Foot did in the 1974 Trade Union and Labour Relations (Amendment) Act. The closed shop had been perfectly legal up until 1971 – it had also been long established in most sections of the press. When journalists too began to demand the post-entry closed shop – particularly as a union-strengthening tactic in the provincial press, where trade union organisation and wage levels are intolerably poor – the proprietors, backed by the tories, started a vicious campaign to prevent it. This has to be seen in a wider context to explain why the proprietors were doubly worried. Things were hotting up in the provincial press for two related reasons. Firstly, an eventual job on a national paper was once the carrot in the provincial press to keep journalists quietly subservient. But Fleet Street's economic crisis and the expansion of the provincial press had put paid to that. Secondly, over the last ten years a steady stream of radicalised graduates has begun to fill the reporters' and sub-editors' desks outside the metropolitan press. Working with the underpaid juniors from school, this has produced a potentially radical and explosive mixture.

The chief fear on the part of editors and proprietors was for what they described as 'editorial freedom'. They feared, for example, that if the editors were forced into the NUJ they would lose their 'independence' and might be subject to the discipline and pressure of the NUJ (as opposed to that of the proprietors and advertisers). For example, situations had arisen in the national provincial NUJ strike in 1974 where numerous papers had continued to appear, staffed by the editor, non-union members and members of the tiny, but extremely employer-oriented Institute of Journalists. Such bold, inventive 'initiatives' might in future be threatened – as well as the editors' 'right' to publish anti-trade union, racist or sexist copy, without any effective comeback.

However, while the rabid, right-wing campaign raged in the national newspapers (many of which ironically had had a real or *de facto* journalists' closed shop for years!) over this threat to 'press freedom', the response of the NUJ has been somewhat inadequate. Instead of taking the 'press freedom' bull by the horns and questioning its assumptions, it retreated into a narrow trade unionism. This weakness was again seen in the latter half of 1977, during the long closed-shop dispute at Darlington. Although the NUJ gave the strikers every support, it was given on the basis of trade unionism alone, thus weakening it. The position of the NUJ and its Executive all along has been to argue that the whole issue of the closed shop has nothing to do with 'press freedom' and that this is a red herring thrown in by the press proprietors. They have consistently argued that the closed shop is simply a matter of making the NUJ a stronger union, to get better wages and so on, which was supposed to be the proprietors' main fear. This was to reduce the whole issue to a purely economistic level, precisely when the proprietors were going on the *political* offensive, using a time-honoured *ideological* weapon. This required a *political* response from the NUJ. Now plans are underway for a 'press charter' intended to guarantee no interference in editorial matters, which most of the NUJ leadership would be happy to sign. Such a charter would mean the effective ditching of the NUJ's code of conduct.

We would argue that what the NUJ ought to have said, not just to the proprietors, but to the whole labour movement, was: 'We haven't got "press freedom", as you all well know, but the closed shop could be one small step towards getting the excellent NUJ code of conduct put into practice – 100 per cent. NUJ membership in the press, including the editor, backed up by the labour movement, is the best means for carrying this out. Yes, we do want to "interfere" with the media – to make them more accountable and responsible to the mass of the working people. Only in that way can we answer in particular the vicious anti-trade union copy, which quite rightly makes the working class unsympathetic to journalists and their union.'

With such a political response, the NUJ would have been in a position to appeal to the labour movement, and particularly the print workers, for support in the closed shop battle. Also, that closed shop battle, fought on such a basis, would have enabled and required journalists to come into contact with other sections of the working class, from whom they are often severely distanced. These contacts and alliances are indispensable, given the NUJ's weakness and specific location in the labour process.

Of course, it is important that any such moves in control and access should not be restricted to the NUJ or the media unions in general. This is precisely the other string to the proprietors' bow – that such bodies represent only a fraction of the population. One can argue that at least they are democratically run bodies (or some of them are!) – unlike the press proprietors – but here again the questions of maximum access and the right of reply become key elements in our strategy.

So in the short- and medium-term, a strategy of direct action by media workers and the broader movement both inside and outside the media is vital. These must take up specific issues of press content, stressing the necessity for greater access and right of reply, to forestall and destroy the whole myth of 'press freedom' as presently constituted.

Another field in which the question of 'press freedom' re-emerges concerns the whole issue of new technology in the printing industry. Here again a strategy based on maximising access and freedom of expression in the press can transform the present defensive struggles going on, against redundancy and 'rationalisation' through the introduction of new electronic forms of typesetting, into an offensive struggle which could gain the sympathy and support of the labour movement. As Marx pointed out, technological innovation, leading to more efficient production methods, has two effects under capitalism: unemployment for many and increased exploitation for those still left at work. Such is the case in the printing industry today – and the print unions, particularly the NGA – are fighting a lone battle against such 'new technology'. But rationally administered, 'new technology' can lead to an extension of the productive forces for the benefit of all, coupled with a shorter working week and easier, healthier working conditions for all print workers. The media unions ought to be arguing for the increased capacity now available on modern setting and printing systems to be put to the service of the community, to give all sorts of groups – trade unions, community groups, political organisations, women's groups and others – access to print, possibly for the first time. Such an extension of access would obviate the need for redundancy and help the print unions draw in wider support for their struggle against the employers' offensive.

In the case of the electronic media, in addition to the strategy we have outlined additional demands and tactics are required. As far as these media are concerned, the working class has the same relation to them, comparatively speaking, as it had to the press 150 years ago. In Britain we face a total *state* monopoly of these media, either in terms of licensing or direct ownership. The labour movement organisations are almost totally excluded from access, except as the long-suffering objects of media coverage. This monopoly must be broken, as a basic democratic necessity which could begin to open up tremendous organisational and educational resources for the mass of the working class. The state defends its monopoly with *technical* arguments – the airwaves need to be allocated sparingly and 'rationally' to prevent interference with emergency services, defence transmissions, etc. But the real reasons are *political* – the bourgeois state recognises the power that these media hold. And the possibilities are evident. During the 1977 firefighters' strike, firemen in South London used their short-wave radios to co-ordinate their pickets for a period, before they were jammed by the local authorities. In Italy, where the state monopoly has been broken, armed state repression was still used against Radio Alice, in Bologna, in April 1977 when the broadcasters tried to help co-ordinate student demonstrators in their battle with police at the university.

These media are an indispensable resource for a developing socialist movement. A city radio station is cheap to set up and run – much cheaper than a press – flexible, immediate, and potentially open to everyone as audience and participants alike. A national network of trade union radio stations would on the whole be more useful than the proposed daily newspaper – and far cheaper too! Television is more expensive, admittedly, but cheaper, and smaller video systems are now coming on to the market. They too could be used to link working-class struggles visually and to exchange and debate tactics and ideas.

Basing ourselves on the precedents in Italy the labour movement and the left must start a campaign for its own radio and television stations, as well as for access for other types of group – women's groups, community groups, black organisations and so on. The state monopoly of the airwaves must be broken once and for all, in the same way that heavy restrictions on the press were fought and ended in the last century. We must force ourselves into the electronic age. To quote Enzensberger again:

> That the Marxist left should argue theoretically and act practically from the standpoint of the most advanced productive forces in their society, that they should develop in depth all the liberating factors immanent in these forces and use them strategically, is not an academic expectation, but a political necessity.[10]

To date that has barely begun to happen.

Chapter 12

Workers' Control and the Media

Dave Bailey

What policy should revolutionary socialists adopt towards the communications media? This is not a new question for the working-class movement. However, the enormous explosion in the communications industry over the last fifty years, the introduction of radio and television in particular, has simply brought it into sharper focus for socialists today.

The introduction of television is one of the most significant technical revolutions ever brought about by capitalism. It has led directly to a many hundredfold increase in the sheer volume of news, information, fiction, documentary material and drama – that is, culture – available to the working class. Virtually no home in the country is now without television. On the other hand television, along with radio and the press, is obviously an aspect of bourgeois state power. Even where not directly owned and run by the state, as in the case of the press and some of the radio stations, the media are tightly controlled by the state and are therefore closely bound up with the maintenance of capitalist society. These two facts pose problems for socialist theory.

The technical revolution represented by television is truly astonishing. Events all over the globe can be beamed more or less instantaneously into the living-room. Controversy and political debate is part of the daily output of television. Party political broadcasts, statements by the government and opposition parties, by heads of ministries and leaders of industry, are accessible immediately all over the country through television. The major political parties address their supporters via television rather than on the street-corner or on the radio, and some, such as the Labour Party, have given up producing a daily newspaper.

At the same time as it amplifies the *political* life of the country, television gives instantaneous access to *other* media forms. The decline in attendance at theatres and cinemas, for example, is not a sign of 'declining cultural standards', as some would have it. On the contrary, many hundreds of hours of drama and film are broadcast each week over the television networks, and at less cost to the viewer. People witness far *more* drama and film than even before. Even that archaic art-form, the novel, has not so much died out, as undergone a reincarnation in the form of the television serial – indeed, television has treated all kinds of novels, from 'pulp' to 'classic', exactly in this way.

Television even seizes whole *institutions* and puts them on the air. Today it is no longer even essential to attend a university to acquire a university degree. It is only necessary to tune into the Open University. Potentially television could render schools themselves unnecessary, at least in their present form. It is ironic that during the present outcry against the alleged decline in standards of literacy in the average British secondary school, it tends to be overlooked that literacy itself is declining in importance. Television brings to an end the equation of ignorance and illiteracy. The child of today may know much more from watching television from an early age than the teacher who has spent his or her life book-bound.

The enthusiasm with which children approach television illustrates one of its secrets: its *audio-visual* nature. This is what makes it simultaneously attractive *and* informative. It does away with second-hand verbal accounts of events and presents a direct visual image, in combination with sound. The present generation of revolutionary socialists was educated about the nature of American imperialism with the assistance of daily television coverage of the war in Vietnam. Today, we can see what socialist revolution in the West will look like, not only by reading second-hand accounts, but by the television pictures direct from Portugal, of demonstrations, mass meetings, occupied factories, fraternisation of soldiers and workers – indeed, what else could the television camera report?

In Britain television has been available to the public for little more than twenty years. That is a very short time. There is no doubt that this explosive technical innovation is still in its infancy. There is equally no doubt that the need of the capitalist class to maintain its power over society comes increasingly into conflict with the technical possibilities of television. This is very obvious when it comes to the question of the number of networks, for instance. Technically, there is no reason whatsoever why there cannot be a far greater number of channels available to the viewer than the three existing ones, or why regional television transmitters must be limited to copying the national network. The reason for these restrictions is political, as are the restrictions on who appears on television. The suppression of the pirate radios – and their replacement by *ersatz* state-approved stations – is a direct expression of the state's desire to maintain its censorious control on the air.

We must now turn to the problems which these radical innovations pose for the labour movement. The working class is a dispossessed class. Consequently it goes into a socialist revolution without having accumulated even a small fraction of the economic, cultural and social resources which the bourgeois class had in the great revolutions of the past. The workers' movement has only its cadres, its political parties, its unions and its solidarity. True, the movement has been able to build up a press of its own. But this press has always been a very poor stepsister to the powerful bourgeois dailies. As to television transmission, this is even more beyond the economic and technical resources of the labour movement. As a result, the seizure of the bourgeois media by the workers' movement has always been an important issue in the revolutionary overturn.

In the German revolution, during the famous Spartacus week of January 1919 in Berlin, the major military action took place in one single street of the city. It was this street which housed the major editorial offices and printing presses of the country's most important daily newspapers. These buildings had all been seized by the revolutionary insurgents and included the editorial offices of *Vorwaerts*, the paper of the Social Democratic Party. Noske's troops had to virtually demolish the street to dislodge the insurgents.

More recently, in the Portuguese revolution of 1974–5, the workers seized Radio Renascenca, which belonged to the Catholic Church, placed it under workers' management and opened the network to workers in struggle, without any attempt to censor the broadcasts. The government of the Armed Forces Movement found this station such a threat that they sent in the military to blow up the radio masts. But no workers' revolution has yet attempted to seize television.

These examples obviously bring us face to face with the problem of state power. A revolution decides which class should hold state power, and therefore which class should have overall control and direction of the media. In future revolutionary situations in Europe, the struggle for the television and radio stations, we can be sure, will play a quite critical role – perhaps more than the press did in the past. So what should our policy towards the control of the networks be, and how does this work itself out in terms of such factors as the content of broadcasts?

To approach this question, it is convenient to divide up the content of the media into two areas. On the one hand, we have the directly political material which the media deals with and processes. This includes newscasts, news analysis, plays on political topics, documentaries, discussions and so on. On the other hand, we have the generality of television productions which, because television is the dominant communications medium and is so universal, reflect the culture of the entire country.

This is not an arbitrary distinction. Of course we know that every cultural production, of whatever sort, embodies certain ideological assumptions which are traceable back to a particular form of society, a particular type of class rule. These are only implicit in most cultural productions and far from obvious to the broad mass of viewers. However, in the sphere of the directly political questions which television handles, the 'class bias' of the media is more obvious. The hand of ruling-class control is more visible. Every trade unionist who discusses the media will invariably remark, for example, on the unchanging hostility of the media towards workers in industrial disputes, no matter what the particular circumstances of the dispute happen to be. It is reasonable to expect – and history proves – that the workers' movement will, generally speaking, intervene in the media first and foremost around the media's treatment of questions that are overtly political. When the workers' movement seizes those apparatuses, it will not do so readily equipped with an alternative set of television programmes to hand or with the means of transforming the culture of the entire country. It will intervene at first, as always in such matters, with a very particular and more limited aim in view.

The take-over of the Renascenca radio station and the *Republica* newspaper, and their placing under workers' management, during the Portuguese revolution are very instructive. The workers were prompted to do this, in both cases, by threatened redundancies: that is, for a quite 'limited' reason. The workers wanted to save their jobs. That was the first aim of the struggle. The workers believed their jobs threatened by the policies being pursued by the management. After all, Portugal had just emerged from the dark age of fascism. The thirst for information, news, knowledge, culture of all kinds, was enormous. So how did it come about, asked the workers, that these enterprises were having to lay off staff?

The workers alleged that Radio Renascenca and the newspaper *Republica* (a pro-Socialist Party newspaper) were adopting 'too narrow' an editorial line. At that time in Portugal you could read, even in the bourgeois newspapers, the statements and even entire programmes of the different political groups. A paper or radio station that failed to combine its own editorial position with such openness of reporting would not attract support. In *Republica* the workers at first demanded that, although the editor would remain free to state his own view in editorials, the other parties of the working class should have the right to place their opinions in the same paper or in another paper printed in the same shop. This was rejected. When the workers seized *Republica* and expelled the old managerial and editorial team, Mario Soares, the Socialist Party leader, claimed that this was an attack on the 'freedom of the press', despite the fact that the Socialist Party had daily access to television and had bigger papers than *Republica*.

In the case of Radio Renascenca, once the workers took it over they opened up the networks to any group of workers in struggle – women's abortion groups and so on – without any editorial censorship. The Catholic Church claimed that this was undermining 'morality' and the 'freedom of the press'. On the contrary, both these actions enormously expanded the freedom of the media and the level of cultural and moral debate in the country – not the purely abstract freedom to *own* a paper or radio station, but the *actual* freedom of unlimited access to these media by wide sections of the population.

Workers in Britain have already had some small experience of workers' management and control in the media. For instance, the workers at Briant Colour Printing set up their plant under workers' management and printed posters for the fight of the Pentonville 5 against the tory government – in a limited way they produced for *use* rather than *exchange*. More recently, print workers have occasionally demanded the right to reply alongside editorials attacking the trade unions, and the right to invigilate over future editorial material. Yet the proprietors of Fleet Street and their accolytes such as Lord Goodman claim that these are attacks on the freedom of the press! What they actually mean is that they, and *only* they, should be free to use the press for their own purposes, merely because they happen to own the paper.

The right of reply in the bourgeois media is a fundamental need of the workers' movement, and prepares the way for an eventual liberation of the media, as at Renascenca and *Republica*. Just imagine what would happen in Britain tomorrow if every group which was attacked and slandered daily in the media had an automatic right to reply! There have been some isolated successes of this tactic already – in October 1976, in the wake of the dismissal of Sir Richard Dobson from British Leyland, Bernard Levin wrote a scurrilous attack on *Socialist Challenge* in *The Times* for publishing Peter Cooper's tape of Dobson's racist after-dinner speech. The editor of *Socialist Challenge*, Tariq Ali, was able to secure a 1200-word reply, by reference to the NUJ's code of conduct, which demands such a 'right' if the issue is of 'sufficient importance'.

If in general the workers had the strength to impose this rule in the whole of the media – for which sooner or later they would require an armed force on their side as the workers in Portugal had – this would establish workers' control over the managers and editors of the media. And what a transformation of the network this control would bring. It would, of course, quickly confront the movement with the need to take state power, to create an overall workers' administration of the media, transform the entire content of the media and open up more networks to allow access to a whole range of previously-excluded groups.

The working class has no interest in depriving anybody of access to media. The workers' slogan must be for the greatest freedom of the press and the air; and the best way to ensure this is to nationalise them and throw them upon. This is a far cry from the 'freedom' represented by the Murdochs and the Beaverbrooks. Even in the heat of sharp political crises, the workers have little to gain, for instance, from censoring government statements – how much more effective that the object of the attack should have equivalent air-time. Only those directly trying to organise civil war against the workers or stir up racist pogroms, as the fascists do, should be censored.

The same principle should be extended to the content of the media in general. This is not a small question. We are dealing here, in the case of television especially, with almost the entire cultural life of the country. Anyone who takes charge of the media will be severely judged on the attitude taken here. The revolutionary movement must have no truck with Stalinist attempts to impose a crude 'proletarian culture' or to 'purge bourgeois culture' from the media.

Of course, we all know that many of the programmes shown on television are bad, indeed harmful. What possible point would be served, however, by trying to censor *Coronation Street* on the grounds that it provides no solution to the problems of working-class domestic life? Or to censor the many quiz programmes on the basis that gambling – which is what these programmes appeal to – expresses the alienation of the working class? If those television programmes which *do* discuss the political and social alternatives (whether in dramatic form or outright polemic) are pushed to minority time slots on television, this reflects the present political and cultural outlook of the working class. This is a material fact which only class struggle and socialist transformation can change.

Naturally, a first step is to provide a much wider range of choices than exists at present – as we have already said, the multi-channel possibilities of television make this possible. Nor is there a shortage of real dramatic, artistic and technical talent in Britain today. Much of it is being destroyed or under-utilised because of the economics of the capitalist system, as they combine with the cultural backwardness of the working class. The Association of Cinematograph, Television and Allied Technicians (ACTT), in an excellent report on the film industry,[1] showed how the British film industry had been pushed aside by the Hollywood industry. In 1970 MGM closed their British studios and became, in effect, distributors for the Hollywood product. The answer, said the ACTT, was not to try to compete with Hollywood (who are not amateurs when it comes to knowing what the mass of cinema-goers want). This would be economically impossible, let alone culturally undesirable. Instead, the industry as a whole should be nationalised and freed from the criteria of profitability. This would make it possible to provide a greater range of film and drama, independent of box-office revenue.

This is an excellent principle. Here, the employment and cultural needs of the working class coincide. However, for the cultural transformation of the working class such as to allow it to exercise state power, it would not be sufficient simply to make available cultural material that treats social questions seriously. Millions of people will decide to reject certain options, such as *Coronation Street* or the quiz shows, in favour of others only if, as a result of their *actual struggles*, they come to ask new questions or, if you prefer, pose the old questions in a different way.

For example, many plays have been produced for television dealing with the problem of the oppression of the housewife. But for millions of housewives to derive real value from them requires them to be actively struggling on those issues (such as abortion and nursery facilities). One of the ways that the media are used to prevent such an interaction taking place is to maintain a black-out on the struggles of the oppressed, or at least to slander and distort them. When we throw the channels open to those in struggle, millions of people will undergo a giant leap forward in their cultural and political development. I do not think that the present schedule of television programmes will survive it for long! But it will be freedom of access, not censorship, that will destroy the present bourgeois culture in the media.

If this essay has one main point, it is just this: the question of the media is, for revolutionary socialists, not a *technical* problem but a *political* one. The appearance of television as a new communications medium does not pose any qualitatively *new* social problem, and it certainly does not solve any old ones. Marshall McLuhan,[2] who claims that television has transformed the world into a 'global village', wants to say by this that the medium itself overcomes political divisions and conflicts, as if these were nothing more than a 'breakdown of communication'. Conversely, on the left, we still find paranoia about the new media which, ironically, is based on the same premiss as McLuhan's argument: that technical forms can overcome the social and economic content of our world. Some on the left want to say that television is a new weapon for the 'integration' of the working class into capitalism – as if the age-old class conflicts of capitalist society could somehow be erased or fail to find their reflection in the media. In many ways the new media reflects – or should we say 'screens' – the class conflicts of society more clearly and sharply than the old. Nor can the media escape the universal contradiction between the technical possibilities contained within it and the property forms within which it is constrained.

These false reactions on the left can lead to what Hans Magnus Enzensberger, in an important article on the media,[3] has called 'cultural archaism'. He quotes as an example the insurgent students in May 1968, who when marching through the streets of Paris in triumph over the CRS (Compagnie de Républican Sécurité) riot-police chose not to seize the radio headquarters but the Odéon Theatre instead, thereby leaving the most important means of communication in the hands of the government. This was clearly a fatal error. The revolution in Europe must not be afraid to seize the *dominant*, the most important, media forms in society. The obstacles in this field are not technical, but *political*. As I have tried to show, however, the political issues raised in seizing the new media, television and radio, are exactly the same as those posed in seizing the old media, the bourgeois press: the questions of 'freedom', 'censorship', workers' control and so on. The new media forms dramatise them, but they do not change them.

It might be as well to say a bit more about the general problem of workers' control. There is much confusion surrounding this question, largely because many people, when speaking about 'workers' control', tend to conflate the *goal* of the movement with the different *means* which will have to be employed to reach the goal. The goal of the movement is to create, within a workers' state, a workers' administration of industry, including the media, based on democratically elected workers' councils. However, the working class does not generally arrive at a workers' state readily equipped with the skills of management, the financing and running of enterprises, and certainly does not arrive equipped with its first Five-Year Plan. The workers will, in many cases, have to undergo a certain period of *apprenticeship* in this field, and for this purpose it will prove useful to enlist the co-operation of as many of the old managerial and technical workers as possible. Naturally, this depends to a large extent on their attitude to the revolution.

However, even where the workers first have to intervene in management over very serious questions – for example, to stop deliberate economic sabotage (as in Chile under Allende or in Russia in 1917) – it by no means follows that the old managerial workers should simply be expelled. The workers do not always have the means to create a workers' management (access to the banks, cultural level and so on) in their place. Thus it may be necessary to have a 'transitional' regime in many of the enterprises in which the old managerial and technical staff are compelled to operate under the vigilant control of the workers. Our attitude to *owners* by contrast is quite uncompromising.[4]

Of course, the workers have not thought all this out in advance. Workers intervene in managerial affairs for concrete reasons, as I have said. In industry, it will most likely be to stop sabotage designed to demoralise the workers, create starvation and so on. In the media, it might well be aimed at putting a stop (through imposing a general right of reply) to increasing reactionary provocation of the workers, designed to pave the way for repression. In taking these concrete actions, however, the workers are led to pose the more general and long-term question of creating a workers' administration for industry and the media.

However, the need for tactical flexibility in this area not only stems from the way in which socialist revolutions unfold and develop (from particular issues to the more general), but is rooted in the inevitable *cultural lag* between the workers and the managerial/technical strata, which capitalist society produces. This does not disappear simply because workers become politically conscious.

Now this is very important. It is sometimes said that the cultural lag between the workers and the managerial/technical strata has grown wider in the past thirty or forty years, with the enormous scientific and technical revolution brought about by electronics. It is indeed true that the working class is confronted by a vast array of highly sophisticated technicians, scientists and administrative and managerial workers of all sorts. But it would be quite wrong to draw from this the impossibility of the workers' movement exercising state power. After all, while electronics have brought about what has been called a 'third industrial revolution', they have revolutionised the media too. Television provides *exactly* the sort of cultural and educational medium which is needed for exercising power today. For with television it is quite simple to present the essentials of a particular discipline, theoretical, applied or practical, to millions of people – instantaneously and in audio-visual form.

The old image of workers spending ten years at school and then having to spend their evenings in libraries in order to acquire a certain cultural level is completely outmoded. Books are no longer the key to the universe. Today, television makes it possible for millions of people to make technically informed decisions about the overall direction of policy in technically sophisticated fields, such as nuclear energy or medical research.

Finally, let me recommend the writings of Ernest Mandel on the question of the media. He is one of the few Marxists today to have thought out the possibilities of the new media. In a recent article in *International*,[5] he makes the remark that socialism in the latter third of the twentieth century means workers' councils, plus automation, plus television. Mandel suggests that television opens up the way, not only for a vast cultural revolution for humankind, but also for a tremendous leap forward in the organisation of workers' democracy. For instance, delegates to national or regional bodies could be watched via televised reports by the people who elected them. If they were seen to deviate from their mandate, they could be subject to instantaneous recall via telephone!

Unlike the Soviet Union we shall not have to construct socialism with people who have barely emerged from the dark ages of pre-literacy but with people already becoming attuned to the possibilities of the new media of the age of post-literacy.

Chapter 13

Culture, the Media and Workers' Democracy

Tariq Ali

It is very easy, when we look at the cultural and political situation in the Soviet Union and eastern Europe today, to get the impression – particularly for those who are not students of history – that such a situation is the *inevitable* result of socialist revolution. Therefore a useful starting point to this essay would be a tribute to those revolutionaries in Russia who, after the Revolution, paid a great deal of attention to problems of culture, problems of the development of art, problems of inculcating in the masses an understanding of such questions. They also took up the issues of socialist freedoms very seriously.

The organisations of the revolutionary left normally concentrate on those features of the Russian Revolution which they regard as more relevant to everyday political discussion, tactics and strategy. This is obviously vital, but it is useful to recall that there was another aspect of that revolution which was also very important and from which we have much to learn. In other words, the Russian Revolution did not merely have the effect of political and economic liberation for the masses. It also attempted to liberate the masses culturally and socially. The hopes that it aroused in its first decade were enormous.

Some of the experiments which took place in that country in a whole range of fields sustained these hopes and showed what could be possible after the overthrow of capitalism. I think that two quotations from two very different leaders of the Russian Revolution will give some flavour of the debates which took place in that period, an insight into the preoccupations of many people at that period. The Revolution was not solely a *narrowly* defined political act. It was obviously and predominantly that in terms of the seizure of power, but much more was at stake. For instance, the first Commissar of Culture, Arts and Education, Lunacharsky, was extremely concerned about a whole range of related questions, such as architecture. So concerned, that at the height of the uprising in 1917, prompted by a false rumour he had heard, he sent the following letter of resignation to the Central Committee of the Bolshevik Party:

> I have just heard from eye-witnesses what happened in Moscow. St Basil's and the Uspensky cathedrals are being destroyed. The Kremlin, where the most important artistic treasures of Petrograd and Moscow are collected, is bombarded. There are thousands of victims. What more can happen? I cannot bear it. My cup is full. I am powerless to stop this awfulness. It is impossible to work under the pressure of thoughts which are driving me mad. That is why I am resigning from SOVNACOM [the council of ministers]. I understand the full gravity of this decision, but I can do no more.[1]

When he found out that St Basil's cathedral had not been bombed, he immediately withdrew his resignation. But this gives an indication of the range of opinion, concern and priority there was within the Bolshevik Party. It was at this time a party led not by philistine, cold-blooded bureaucrats but by internationalist revolutionaries, intensely cultured and speaking a number of European languages. And Lunacharsky was not an unimportant revolutionary leader.

The second quotation is from Trotsky and provides us with a further glimpse of that immediately post-revolutionary period (though this expression of those vital lessons was not written until 1938). Trotsky polemicised throughout the 1920s and 1930s against those who believed that only a proletarian culture – a 'culture' which initially bore little resemblance to the socialist realism of Stalin, incidentally – was the solution to pressing cultural problems (see Carl Gardner's essay in this volume on this debate). Trotsky wrote:

> To those who urge us whether for today or for tomorrow to consent that art should submit to a discipline which we hold to be

radically incompatible with its nature, we give a flat refusal and repeat our intention of standing by the formula 'freedom for the arts'. We recognise of course that the revolutionary state has a right to defend itself against a counter-attack from the bourgeoisie, even when it draps itself in the flag of science or art, but there is an abyss between those enforced and temporary measures of revolutionary self-defence and the pretensions to lay commands on artistic creation. If for the better development of the forces of material production the revolution must build a socialist regime of centralised control, to develop intellectual creation an anarchist regime of individual liberty must from the first be established. No authority, no dictation, not the least trace of orders from above. Only on the basis of friendly co-operation without constraint from outside, will it be possible for scholars and artists to carry out their tasks which will be more far-reaching than ever before in history.[2]

In a curious way these two very different characters, Lunacharsky and Trotsky, express in these two quotations the mood of the Russian Revolution. In the first few years after the Revolution it was this mood which dominated in a whole number of fields, particularly in the field of art, theatre and literature. Lunacharsky at one point had a furious argument with Lenin: at the height of the paper shortage Lunacharsky wanted to print tens of thousands of copies of the latest book of Mayakovsky's poems. Lenin said that maybe a few thousand should be printed as there were more urgent things for the press to print. Lunacharsky delivered a stinging rebuke to the 'philistines' and finally had his way. Lenin lost that argument and Mayakovsky was printed in tens of thousands of copies.

Today if you look at the Soviet Union, or even the bulk of the revolutionary left in the West, these debates seem totally bizarre. And yet they are very important, very creative and represent something of what we are fighting for.

As for the Russian press, newspapers such as *Isvestia* – the newspaper of the soviets – were open to all political currents which operated in the soviets. *Pravda* – the newspeper of the Central Committee of the Bolsheviks – was none the less full of public discussion and debate, even at the height of the civil war.[3] Even before the civil war, in the war against Germany when the treaty of Brest–Litovsk was being considered, there was a big division within the Central Committee (with Lenin in a minority of two). But all these vital debates were being conducted in the pages of *Pravda*. Some enterprising publisher should commission someone to reproduce these early debates in *Pravda*, which are very rich and a million miles away from what happened later.

In the field of dramatic creations, too, new techniques were involved – Meyerhold's plays used to attract thousands of workers. They attempted to depict on stage, in a non-naturalistic manner, the reality that was transpiring before the very eyes of the working masses themselves, at the height of the civil war. During the performances messengers from the battle-front used literally to come into the mass theatres and march straight on to the stage to read the latest reports from the front. When victories were reported the plays were interrupted and celebrations took place. Also there were things like the mass re-creations and re-enactments on the streets of historic events like, in 1921, the re-enactment of the 1917 storming of the Winter Palace, using a cast of 20,000 workers brought in from the factories.

In other words, there were very challenging developments taking place in the arts side by side with more traditional forms – one was not counterposed to the other. There is insufficient space to discuss the process which led to the degeneration of the Russian Revolution, but all this was finished by the late 1920s. By the 1930s a new centralised cultural apparatus was in full swing. The Stalinisation which took place in the political parties and the soviets was also extended to the field of information, where a total state monopoly was established. That is the defining characteristic of all these post-capitalist regimes – that the state is for the total monopoly of information. We must be for the breaking of that monopoly because we argue that it is bureaucratic, arbitrary, undemocratic and leads inevitably to the depoliticisation of the working masses in these societies.

Before I deal with this question, especially what socialists and Marxists should be in favour of, I want to give a few more examples from elsewhere. Revolutions which took place after the Russian Revolution were not as enterprising as the Russian model. This is especially true of the Chinese revolution, which curiously enough, while it liberated a large bulk of humanity from the fetters of feudalism, did not emancipate them culturally. In fact with the success of the revolution there was from the beginning an extremely bureaucratic regime established in the arts.

A monopoly of information has also existed from the beginning in Vietnam. While most of us were totally in solidarity with the struggle of the Vietnamese against the Americans – many of us took part in the big mobilisations and celebrated the Vietnamese victory – we must be totally aware of another feature. It is a feature which really expresses the contradictions of those regimes in the following way: *the press in Saigon today is less free than it was under the puppet regime of Thieu*! In other words the bulk of the population of Saigon had more information facilities under the heavy censorship of Thieu than they do now. And that regime is a revolutionary regime in terms of its overthrow of capital and the defeat of imperialism. That is precisely the dilemma to which we have to address ourselves and which we have to analyse and provide solutions for. The central question remains: 'Is such a state of affairs necessary?'

Before I answer that, I want to give another example which was not totally like the Russian experience but on the other hand was very unlike the experiences of China, Vietnam and eastern Europe, and that is the example of Cuba. Cuba was the first 'television revolution': the first revolution that took place at a time when television existed. Television was widely used in Cuba in the period upto and after the revolution – the Cuban masses related to television as a very important section of the media. Fidel Castro used this medium extremely creatively. If you study the history of the Cuban revolution in the phase when it was in transition from an anti-imperialist revolution to socialist revolution you will see the role that television played. You will see how Fidel used television speeches to inculcate a political consciousness in the masses.

Also the Cuban press, which was under the control of individual capitalists, was not touched for a whole period by the Fidelista regime. For one reason – Fidel grasped a very important point which is worth learning: the masses do not learn simply from the revolution (though of course they do). In certain circumstances they also learn from and develop a new consciousness from their experience of the counter-revolution. In other words the capitalist press's attacks on the revolution, their distortion of what was going on – developments which the masses identified with – was a much better way of confronting them with the nature of the press than a blanket suppression.

What began to happen in Cuba was that the printing workers used to insert under all the items they thought were wrong what they called 'revolutionary tails'. They didn't censor them, they didn't stop their publication. If a capitalist paper in Cuba had an editorial saying the Cuban leadership was doing this or that, that Fidal is a rogue or whatever, you could read it and then at the bottom of the paragraph the printing workers in that particular press would insert a 'tail' which said: 'This is completely wrong. We disagree 100 per cent with what the leader-writer has written. It does not express our views.' It was a limited intervention in that they were not in a position to demand from the newspaper a full page to express their views. But nonetheless it showed a correct way of dealing with the problem and one which educated the masses.

Also there was a big political debate between the newspaper of the Cuban Communist Party and the newspaper of the July 26 Movement on the road to take. There was a big theoretical debate in the journals, in particular *Critical Thought*, between different currents. For example, there was a debate between Bettelheim and Mandel in this journal in the period immediately following the Cuban revolution. Bettelheim defended one wing of the Cuban leadership and Mandel defended Che Guevara's positions on the running of the economy.

In the field of culture, too, there were big developments – not as significant as the Russian innovations but nonetheless big developments. Some of the best Cuban films were made in the early period of the revolution and big discussions took place on, for instance, television. If you see the book of Cuban posters[4] produced in this period you get some idea of what was taking place. Unfortunately one has to say that this ended in 1967–8 – *Critical Thought* was closed down – but it went on for a long time. Nevertheless it is still not the same as China or many of the east European countries. The level of debate is still more lively, but a monopoly of information, albeit more flexible, has now been imposed in that country.

Another example is closer to us in Europe and that is the example of the Prague Spring, 1968 – the situation which existed in Czechoslovakia before the tanks went in. All the reporters who went to Czechoslovakia in this period came back absolutely traumatised – even reporters from British bourgeois newspapers. They came back traumatised because they saw that the Czech press was the freest in Europe, east or west. They had never seen so many debates taking place in the bourgeois press in western Europe. And the Czech press from January to August 1968 debated *everything*. They had debates

on politics, they had debates on economics and the newspaper of the
Young Communist League had even begun to serialise the works
of Isaac Deutscher. A whole number of new openings were taking
place, in the cultural field, the literary field and the political field. It
was a real 'spring'. It had its limitations but there is no doubt that
these debates and discussions took place.

If you look, too, at Czech television, a remarkable transformation
took place. From being a boring, dogmatic organ of Party propaganda which no one watched except when a western film was being
shown, television became the most vigorous in Europe. For the first
time people began to switch on to watch political debates. They had a
programme of one hour every evening in which those who had been
the political victims and prisoners of the Stalinist regime – many of
them genuine Communists – were allowed to recount their experiences and then interrogate those who had persecuted them. The
lawyers who had prosecuted them and the warders who had tortured
them were brought to the television studio to be put in the front seat.
You can imagine the impact that has on political consciousness. One
victim asked a warder: 'Look, you tortured me very badly. Now why
did you do it?' What could the person say? He gave the classical reply
of people in this position: 'It wasn't us. We were simply obeying
orders.' So then a debate took place – who gave the orders, why were
they given? And a real purge from below began to take place of people
who had given such orders. Things began to come out in the open.
And through this openness, the Czech Communist Party became the
most popular Communist Party in the world.

If you look at the newsreels of May Day 1968 in Prague, you'll see
an amazing sight. You'll see a spontaneous political demonstration.
You'll see banners, some of them right-wing, some of them very left-
wing, some of them demanding more freedom, more liberties, some
of them carrying portraits of Dubček, some carrying portraits of
Guevara. You'll see revolutionary Marxist literature being distributed. There was a manifesto distributed by Czech revolutionaries
saying that Dubček had not gone far enough – that the process
needed taking further towards the institutionalisation of socialist
democracy. The weakness of the Prague Spring was that the debates
took place only in the Communist Party press. There was, however, a
big discussion taking place about the right of other parties outside the
Communist Party to exist. Who knows what would have happened?
The Czech Communist Party, during the Spring, was the first

Communist Party to recognise the rights of tendencies and factions to exist within it. This is a very important right because, if you accept that, it is very difficult to refuse that right to other 'external' political parties. One of the key elements used by Stalin to smash all those opposed to him was the ban imposed on tendencies and factions inside the Bolshevik Party in 1921 – a ban supported by all the central leaders of the Party, including Lenin and Trotsky. It was meant to be a temporary ban but it became permanent. It has still never been lifted. It was used to smash all opposition to Stalin and incipient Stalinism. In Prague in 1968 for the first time in the Communist movement since then, we saw this ban lifted and a week later the tanks went in.

The tanks went in not because Dubček and the Czech government were negotiating a deal with the West Germans or the Americans or anyone else. Not because of those stupid reasons given by the Soviet government, who could not find any evidence of the restoration of capitalism – there was never any chance of that. The main reason was the example which Czechoslovakia was creating. And the thing which really frightened them was that in the Ukraine, Ukrainian printing workers wanted their own newpaper, printed in Ukrainian, to put forward their political arguments. They could not print it because of the state monopoly, so what did they do? They sent a delegation of Ukrainian militants across the border to Czechoslovakia to make an appeal to the print workers' union there to print the newspapers. They did and pledged to do so fairly regularly. This was a real challenge to the power of the central bureaucracy in the Soviet state. They could not deal with it *politically* – by debate and discussion – so in went the tanks.

The reason I have spent some time giving these examples is to get away from the idea that monolithism, one-party statism, a total stranglehold on ideas and a monopoly of information, is the norm or should be the norm. It is at present, but it should not be. We already have in the history of the worker's movement experiences which can be and will be developed, particularly when we talk about revolutions in western Europe. We are living in countries where bourgeois democracy exists. Bourgeois democracy is not entirely a fake, because it is based on the partial *consent* of the masses. A very important part of this democracy is that the masses have basic rights to meet and organise. They are restricted, there are all sorts of constraints put on them, but within bourgeois democracy, mass political working-class organisations, trade unions, revolutionary Marxist currents and so on are allowed to exist, to function and to meet.

So revolutionaries in the west face a very particular problem, which is precisely that the only democracy which the masses know *is* bourgeois democracy. Now, it's no good to say to them that we are in favour of socialist democracy in the future. They'll say, 'Good, but where is it, where does it exist now?' If you talk to serious working-class militants who are not Marxists but are interested in discussing with you, they always ask whether there is any society in the world today where there is socialist democracy. And one is forced to reply in the negative. And it is one thing to say this to workers who are sympathetic to you. You can imagine the impact on mass working-class consciousness of the lack of socialist democracy in China, eastern Europe, Russia, the lot. It is a big problem. And therefore the revolutionary movement has to be extremely sensitive and clear on this question of democracy. We are not going to win the working class in western Europe away from bourgeois democracy, unless they are convinced that the system they are fighting for is going to be more democratic, not less democratic, than that they have already. Who can blame them?

The recent example of Portugal stares us straight in the face. And the *Republica* affair there was the embodiment of the problem. The whole *Republica* affair was handled in a very tactically inept way by the workers in that print shop – that mistake was a central feature which enabled Soares to start a big offensive on the question of 'democracy'. The fact that the workers acted in such a way indicated the lack of revolutionary education on the question of democracy in that country. Given that they had been under fascism for fifty years, this was a bit surprising. Of course Soares used all sort of untruths and demagogy, but the basic facts could not be denied. *Republica* was a paper sympathetic to the Socialist Party – and the workers were mainly members of the far-left groups (not the Communist Party). Instead of taking away and thus censoring that paper, as they did, the Cuban 'model', explained earlier, would have been a far more suitable tactic to deal with the demagogy of social democracy.

The print workers should have told the editor: 'We disagree with the Socialist Party, with its attacks on the workers and so-called "anarchy" etc. However, we recognise that you have a perfect right to put them out, as they do represent the views of the Socialist Party. But we are going to put in two extra pages or take away one page, to publish our views on these questions.' That would have been a much better tactic.

One small group in Portugal – the Liga Communista Internacionalista – did distribute a leaflet to the *Republica* workers at the time, saying precisely this. It had little influence. They were the only group who half-realised the use to which this affair would be put by the right. Soares indeed did go on the offensive on the questions of 'democracy' and 'freedom of the press', ably supported by social democrats the world over. This does not mean that if this had not happened, everything in Portugal would have automatically gone in a different direction. But this incident – despite the support it generated on the left – did make it very easy for Soares and proved ultimately counter-productive to the struggle.

The point here is that the revolutionary left in Portugal, in its majority, totally underestimated the correct democratic instincts of the working class. When Soares got up and said, 'We are in favour of socialist democracy but the Communist Party and the groups of the left are not', they could not provide any answer. He utilised the east European model to mislead the masses and channel sections of them behind bourgeois democracy. We have to state continually that the socialism we are fighting for entails the right for all political parties to exist, and to have their own newpapers, guaranteed by the socialist state.

It is not a Marxist position to deny freedom of expression to any political party, even of the bourgeoisie. Lenin makes the point that the Bolsheviks did not throw the Cadets out of the Soviet; they actively joined the counter-revolution and thus excluded themselves. Lots of people ask us whether we would ban the Conservatives after a revolution. It depends; it's not a question of principle. In normal circumstances, with no foreign intervention, if there was such a bourgeois tendency which wanted the restoration of capitalism, it should have every right to say so. Margaret Thatcher and Keith Joseph could go down to the factory gates at 7 a.m. to sell their papers, appealing to the workers to restore capitalism. However, if there was a NATO military intervention and the tories mobilised to support that intervention, and participated in the civil war to overthrow the workers' state, that is a totally different situation. But in a normal situation, we do have to say that we stand for the rights of even bourgeois tendencies to exist.

Then for people who are not organised into political parties, you would have to establish certain criteria. If, say, a group came to the central printing corporation with 5000 signatures to produce a newspaper or political journal which dealt exclusively with the problem of minority nationalities, or old people, a section of the women's movement, or gay currents or whatever, they should be allowed to do so. Lenin conceived the process in that way – there are numerous quotations from him where he laid down precisely these criteria. And such journals and their distribution would be guaranteed.

The same process would apply to television and radio, if such groups had not the resources to set up a station themselves. In this field we have something to learn from some contemporary capitalist situations in Europe. The Dutch have probably the most advanced television set-up – and are probably the most advanced in this sphere in the whole of Europe. All journals over a certain circulation are automatically granted television time. Those with a circulation over a higher figure are even entitled to set up their own channel. Several organisations and institutions in Holland have their own channel on Dutch *state* television. Admittedly in their case, the process has meant the closer integration of the monopoly press companies with the electronic media, which under capitalism can be restrictive, but the broad principle is one we can learn from.

So also in Italy you can see a situation developing where anyone can set up a television or radio station.[5] Stripped of the domination of capital and the law of the market, such a freedom is something which we could use and guarantee. Any other form of socialist democracy is not democracy at all.

One of the tragedies of the present is that the dead weight of Stalinism has hung for so long on the shoulders of the working-class movement that we have all been infected with it. Its effect has been felt even within the far-left groups. This is closely related to the question of how revolutionary organisations function internally, how their newspapers look, the state of debate in their press and the basis of expulsions from such parties. Most groups tend to be parodies of Lenin's organisation in Czarist Russia, which existed in conditions of virtual clandestinity. It means that their conceptions are totally unrelated to the society in which they are working and the political consciousness of the working class. The point is that democratic rights have to be institutionalised within socialist organisations and all socialist activity. In a very literal sense, in cultural and media questions this means allowing a hundred flowers to bloom and refusing to allow this party or the state to nip these flowers in the bud if it feels that they go against the party which happens to exercise power.

The related point which it is necessary to make is the following: the revolutionary movement in the west today tends to have a very vulgar and philistine attitude to culture and the arts and a very narrow concept of what politics is. This is not uniformly the case, but in general it applies certainly in the Anglo-Saxon countries. The narrowness of this concept can be seen in its press, the indicator of what the revolutionary movement is today. And that is extremely unfortunate. I think those of us who are members of revolutionary organisations have to wage a consistent struggle against this narrowness. The reason is not just that it is nice in the abstract, but is related to the evident fact that the masses in bourgeois society today relate more, in one sense, to television than they do to parliament. More working class people watch a television soap-opera than read a report of yesterday's parliamentary proceedings in the pages of *The Times*, the *Guardian* or the *Daily Mirror*. In other words, the existence of television in the home of most working-class families has had a real impact on working-class consciousness.

This impact is contradictory in the sense that it gives the state a direct interventionist medium in the house of every working-class family, which helps it to atomise working-class consciousness. Its positive feature is that it does broaden – not in a very sophisticated way, but without any doubt it does broaden – the cultural horizons of the working class. Also, in a sense, it internationalises politics. Even though the news in Britain is probably the worst, the most trivialised, in western Europe, nonetheless when a massive struggle takes place in France or Italy or Spain, it is brought home very directly.

And the attitude of the far left – to distrust the media and to say it is all rubbish – is in my view a very philistine attitude. Because in a bourgeois democracy you do have even within the media certain progressive developments. They are not everyday developments, admittedly – they can't be everyday developments in a capitalist society. But you do see occasionally things like *Days of Hope*. You also have the situation where one episode of *Bill Brand* by Trevor Griffiths brought home and explained the question of the Prevention of Terrorism Act to millions of people in one evening better than all the far-left groups put together could possibly have done. We have to relate to these problems, try and analyse them.

It is our analysis that, during the revolutionary process, situations of 'dual power' will develop, with organs of workers' power parallel to and opposed to the bourgeois state organs. In that situation control of television and radio will be absolutely vital. Such control does not determine the outcome, but it plays a very important role. In such a situation and leading up to it, the organisation of media workers from different left-wing groups to discuss such problems is a very important task. In May 1968 in France, in French television, left-wing journalists and media workers were sacked during or after the strike with no response whatsoever from the technicians working there. This indicates the importance such preliminary organisation, even today, can play.

After a socialist revolution, too, the uses to which television can be put to raise mass consciousness, to keep the masses involved in the everyday working of the political system, are enormous. In that sense television has an enormous potential which could be exploited in the interests of the broad working masses after a socialist revolution. One of the big problems after a revolution is keeping the masses involved in the everyday running of the state. The classical answer that they will participate by election to workers' councils is correct, but television will play a very important part in this process in enabling workers from different areas to participate, albeit indirectly, in meetings which are taking place in different parts of the country or even in different parts of the world. Television could enable workers to listen to both sides of the political argument when big debates are taking place. In other words, instead of television being an alienating and atomising force, it could become a force to unite the working class and keep its political consciousness at a very high pitch. Those are some of the problems and some of the potentialities which exist.

The central problem, however, is grasping the point about socialist democracy.[6] Revolutions are going to be impossible without a very vigorous socialist democracy to convince the masses that a very different regime, a more democratic regime, is going to exist after a socialist revolution. This is why questions of the media, of the freedom of those media, the question of rights for minorities and political organisations are questions of supreme importance.

Chapter 14

Mass Media after Capitalism: towards a Proletarian Culture?

Carl Gardner

> Art can turn corners so much more rapidly than Policy. Use it as a
> ferret, not as a four for pulling the State Coach – nobler as the
> second role sounds.
>
> John Berger[1]

In the first five years after the revolution in the Soviet Union, a fierce
debate raged in the leading bodies of the government and the press
over the status of what was called 'proletarian culture'. This was one
of the many debates on policy of all sorts which Tariq Ali alludes to
elsewhere in this volume. Unfortunately that debate was not
terminated by experiment and practice (where all such discussions
ought to be resolved) but by the deadening hand of Stalinist
orthodoxy, which within a decade had imposed 'socialist realism' by
state edict over all fields of cultural work. I want to resurrect that
debate.

What relevance does a fairly arcane discussion in the Soviet Union
over fifty years ago have for contemporary theory and practice? An
examination of that debate, in the light of modern developments,
throws considerable light in three main areas. Firstly, the relationship
between technology and social change and the tempo of development

in post-capitalist societies. Secondly, the assumptions underlying the orthodox Leninist view of cultural questions. Thirdly, related to this, the reassessment of the relationship between so-called 'super-structural' questions, such as culture, and the economic and social 'base'.

But first it is necessary to summarise that debate for those not acquainted with it. The theory of 'proletarian culture' was advanced by a school of writers and poets organised around a journal called *Na Postu*. The chief proponents were figures such as Bogdanov, Lebedinsky, Pletnev, Tretyakov and others. They clamoured for official recognition and adoption by the Soviet state and received much sympathy and support from Bukharin and from Lunacharsky, Commissar of Culture, Arts and Education. The 'Proletcult', as they were dubbed, claimed that the Russian Revolution had ushered in a period where it was possible to develop a truly vanguard 'proletarian culture'. A corollary of this view was an iconoclastic tendency which wished to downgrade or abolish all vestiges of bourgeois art. This view was very much in tune with strong philistine currents, best represented by sections of the peasantry, who had often burnt the libraries and art galleries of their masters during the expropriations of the land. Such extreme, iconoclastic tendencies have been seen in all revolutionary situations, notably amongst the anarchists in Spain during 1936–7.

Lenin and Trotsky both had reason to polemicise against the Proletcult and their views have been handed down to succeeding generations of revolutionary Marxists as the last word on the question. Trotsky in particular took up the debate in a very thorough way. He designated this tendency as corresponding to an impatient, petit-bourgeois intelligentsia, which imagined it could sweep away vast expanses of culture or create new ones, simply by an exercise of the voluntaristic will. In the Preface to *Literature and Revolution* he writes:

It is fundamentally wrong to oppose proletarian to bourgeois culture. Proletarian culture and art will never exist. The proletarian regime is temporary and transitory. Our revolution derives its historic significance and moral greatness from the fact that it lays the foundation for a classless society and for the first truly universal culture.[2]

As hard-headed materialists, both Lenin and Trotsky firmly understood that a socialist society (particularly one being built on the foundations of backward Russia) would depend on all the gains made by bourgeois culture and science for some considerable time. At the end of that period one would have a classless society – socialism, on a world scale – and thus 'proletarian culture' would be inconceivable.

Again Trotsky, in his inimitable style, expresses this conception:

> We are still soldiers on the march. We have a day of rest. We must wash our shirts, cut and brush our hair, and first of all clean and grease our rifles. All our present economic and cultural work is nothing but an attempt to bring ourselves into some sort of order between two battles and two marches . . . Our epoch is not the epoch of a new culture. We can only force open the gate to it. In the first instance, we must acquire the most important elements of the old civilisation.[3]

Trotsky pointed out to the Proletcult that the contribution of the proletariat to literature and art to date had been negligible, and would continue to be negligible. What achievements there were certainly owed their origins to an apprenticeship with bourgeois or 'pre-bourgeois' poets. He described it as a 'piece of populist demagogy' to treat such writings as epoch-making art. The Proletcult spent much of its time baiting the various 'bourgeois' schools, such as the Imagists, the Futurists and the Formalists. Without these works, Trotsky concluded, Soviet literature would be utterly impoverished. These views were based on a realistic view of a society with no great accretions of culture, bourgeois or otherwise. Trotsky saw the need for a long, hard struggle, using all the gains of bourgeois culture. He recognised the material limitation of widespread illiteracy and lack of a written culture, which was the cornerstone of any advanced, technological society. Hence his condemnation of the Proletcult as idealist, ultra-left dreamers.

Within the confines of the Soviet situation in the 1920s – a backward, isolated society – Lenin and Trotsky were undoubtedly correct. But that is not the last word. It is by no means certain that such a position can necessarily be carried over wholesale into the modern, technologically developed, literate democracies with equal applicability. Although the conceptions advanced against the Proletcult do in part stem from an orthodox, programmatic view of the role of the 'dictatorship of the proletariat', they are much more based on a specific, analytical recognition of the needs of an impoverished society with a low cultural and technological level. They do not constitute immutable revolutionary principles – we can see the specific way that concrete historical/social factors determined their necessarily partial view.

The other motive behind Lenin's and Trotsky's hostility to the conception of Proletcult was what they saw as its implicit, and often explicit, anti-peasant character. The peasantry constituted over 80 per cent of the Soviet population and the necessity of making a permanent alliance with them, winning them over to active support for the revolution, was always uppermost in Bolshevik thinking. Here again a genuine socio-economic recognition of the specific nature of Soviet society governed Lenin and Trotsky's cultural assessment.

Because those views were developed in such a socially impoverished climate, it ought not to be surprising that they are inadequate for dealing with a complex, contemporary social formation like Britain. To explain this further, it is necessary first to examine the underlying premises of the Proletcult's positions and those of Lenin and Trotsky. In particular, their implicit views of the relationship between 'culture' and the social/economic formation as a whole. In doing so we will expose a weakness which has run through all of the Marxist tradition, with the partial and notable exception of Gramsci.

If we look firstly at the Proletcult we can see a very clearly articulated view of the relationships between the different elements within the social formation as whole. It is for this reason, and because of the evident ludicrousness of their position, that they are so easy to polemicise against. For them 'culture', provided it is invested with a particular class-content, can play a vanguard role in dragging society as a whole, and presumably the economic and technological elements within it, forward towards socialism. This had its ultimate expression twenty years later in Lysenko's 'proletarian science'. 'Proletarian culture' in their view, voluntaristically imposed, thus becomes a motor-force, superseding and riding roughshod over previous cultural legacies. This part of the 'superstructure' does not just maintain a relative autonomy, but becomes instead a super-determinant. Any consideration of the actual conditions obtaining at the economic base – which classically determines 'in the last instance' – is foregone.

Trotsky and Lenin attacked this position, but the view they

advanced in its place, although much more grounded in an appreciation of material reality, and much less dangerous, is itself inadequate, particularly today. In polemicising against the 'prescriptive' theories of the Proletcult, they admittedly foreshadowed the dangers of the state-prescribed doctrine of 'socialist realism' ten years later. Understandably, since that date specific treatment of cultural work by Marxists has been tainted with the implicit accusation of Zhadnovism[4] – the attempt to equate all cultural productions directly with a particular political line. Such is the level of literary criticism and debate in China to this day.

But what is remarkable about the writing of Lenin and Trotsky, as opposed to the Proletcult, is that there is *no articulation whatsoever* of the relationship between culture and the social formation as whole (that is, the role that cultural production could play within it). Instead theorisation of these very important questions is replaced by a vapid, *laissez-faire* libertarianism. This is expressed in the long quotation from Trotsky in Tariq Ali's essay in this volume and in the following:

> Art must find its own road . . . The methods of Marxism are not its methods. The party exercises leadership in the working-class but not over the (entire) historical process. There are some fields in which it leads directly and imperiously. There are other fields in which it supervises . . . and still others where it can offer its co-operation. There are finally fields where it can only orientate itself and keep abreast with what is going on. The field of art is not one in which the party is called on to command.[5]

This was compounded in the polemic with those sections of the Proletcult who believed that Marxism itself constituted the 'proletarian culture'. Something akin to this is not rare on the left today. Trotsky disabused them of this idea by pointing out correctly that Marxism had been the product, as well as the negation, of bourgeois thought. But in making this point he also admits that so far Marxism had applied its dialectics mainly to economics and politics, whereas culture is 'the sum total of knowledge and skill which characterizes society as a whole, or at least its ruling class'. He does not say whether he thinks it desirable for historical materialism to tackle the cultural sphere, though the implications of the various quotations are that he does not. Somehow culture becomes another, autonomous area, necessarily not susceptible to a materialist analysis and understanding. This separation – although partly in reaction to the Proletcult and implicit Zhadnovism – is a curious position for a thoroughgoing materialism interested in forming an understanding of *and a practice within* the social totality.

The weakness becomes most severe when actually considering the position of those involved in 'cultural production' of any kind. The positions advanced by Trotskyist and Leninist orthodoxy – although far preferable, obviously, to the exclusive precriptions of the Proletcult or socialist realism – do not enable revolutionaries to participate or intervene consciously in the processes of cultural production. In fact, they would seem to preclude it – for implicit within this position is a refusal to elaborate a materialist analysis of the relations between specific modes of cultural production and the development of the revolutionary process within the social formation as a whole. Surely we need some sort of materialist analysis to orient ourselves in a world of myriad artistic/cultural currents and ideas? Any possibility of conscious, planned participation in this process is ruled out for orthodox Leninists – blind chance would seem to rule in this sphere, as in no other.

This is one of the reasons why the revolutionary left has never had much to say to artists or other cultural workers – a line of 'do your own thing, let a hundred flowers bloom and it'll all come out right in the end' is unlikely to help those cultural workers who are moving towards revolutionary politics. Admittedly they don't want rigid prescription, but they do require some elaboration of how the whole complex of social practices under the rubric of 'cultural struggle' – including their own – can help bring about socialism.

The other related phenomenon flowing from this unquestioned orthodoxy is, paradoxically enough, the extreme philistinism of the revolutionary left on these questions. As a result of Trotsky's *laissez-faire* libertarianism (which was itself a healthy response to current developments at the time), coupled with Marxism's chronic failure to elaborate an adequate model of the relative autonomy and *efficacy* of 'superstructural' factors in general and art/culture in particular, the left has simply ignored such questions. The left and its leaderships have drawn the conclusion that such questions are secondary, unimportant or simply irrelevant. 'Let's get on with the class struggle, instead.' From Trotsky's healthy – if incomplete – formulations has come an extreme apathy and ignorance, which he would have abhorred. If these are not party questions in the usual sense of having a 'line' – which indeed they are not – then they cannot be worth considering. Or at least, that is the common conclusion. Again, there is confusion between the rigid prescriptivism of the Stalin school and the necessity to have a *general framework* within which to operate, which explains the relation of cultural production to the social and revolutionary process as a whole.

There are, however, several practical implications of the orthodox view. Firstly, many opportunities are missed effectively to present revolutionary ideas in a form developed from progressive work being done in the cultural field – film and photomontage are examples which immediately spring to mind. But, secondly, and more insidiously, widespread ignorance of cultural theory simply means that undigested and unexamined bourgeois notions are smuggled in through the 'cultural back door'. The almost universal attachment to reactionary forms of bourgeois 'naturalism' is one symptom of this. Another, directly related to this point, is the common belief that art somehow 'reflects' reality. A third example would be the supposition that 'form' or technique is 'neutral' and simply a means to express 'content'. All these ideas, although emergent in the cultural sphere – and thus presumed to be harmlessly separate from politics – have serious political repercussions.

I shall end this section by referring to the analogy made by John Berger in the opening quotation. Although that analogy may express something of the relation of cultural work to the building of socialism, the point remains that even the 'ferret' must have some clear idea *why* it's going down the hole. Otherwise it may come back with a stick – or an unexploded mine – instead of a rabbit.

* * *

To return to the original debate over the status of Proletcult, we have examined the premises, but what were the points at issue? What was it really about? It obviously concerned the rate of development of post-capitalist societies and, within that process, the impact of technology. It was also about the application of the law of combined and uneven development to 'superstructural' elements, such as culture and the arts. These themes are brought out in the attacks on Trotsky by Bukharin at the Bolshevik Central Committee in February 1925. Bukharin accused Trotsky of imagining that the transition to socialism would be of so short a duration that the proletariat would not have time to acheive cultural preponderance and impart its own class character in the cultural field during the last epoch of class society. He was accused of not taking into account the 'unequal tempo' of social and political development in different countries, which in the possibly prolonged period of the dictatorship of the proletariat, before the international revolution was completed, might permit/force it to establish a culture peculiar to it.

This debate was of course a 'shadow' of the much more central disagreement between Bukharin/Stalin's conceptions of 'socialism in one country' and Trotsky's conception of 'permanent revolution', the outcome of which was to scar Soviet society and the world socialist movement to this day. Trotsky did indeed under-rate the duration of the proletarian dictatorship and the extent to which it would acquire a bureaucratic character. Nevertheless this evident mistake does not invalidate his argument against 'proletarian culture'. The era of transition did last longer than Trotsky envisaged but within the Soviet Union it did not make that period any more culturally productive or creative. One could certainly argue that it made it less so.

The truth is that Stalinism did not beget any distinctive proletarian culture, but was involved instead in a process which Isaac Deutscher describes as 'primitive cultural accumulation'. We have seen the rapid and extensive spread of mass education and the progressive accumulation of Western technology – including communications technology. This has simply represented the socially required absorption of the heritage of bourgeois and pre-bourgeois civilisation, not the creation of a qualitatively advanced new culture. It is now more and more the bureaucratic stranglehold on those resources which prevents their democratic deployment and a massive explosion in their liberating potential. In this sense the Soviet Union exhibits some of the same characteristics as contemporary capitalism, as we shall see.

Trotsky understood some of this during the debate with the Proletcult, when he wrote the following startlingly perceptive thesis:

> The bourgeoisie assumed power when it was fully armed with the culture of its time. The proletariat assumes power when it is fully armed only with its acute need *to obtain access to culture*.[6] [Emphasis added]

It is this concept of 'obtaining access to culture', involving particular modes of consumption or assimilation, which is vital when considering contemporary, capitalist societies.

As an aside, one could extend Trotsky's observation as a justification and rationale for cultural work as part of the revolutionary process. One could amend Trotsky to read: 'The proletariat assumes power when it is armed *with its recognition* of its acute need to obtain access to culture.' In other words, part of the aim of revolutionary cultural work should be precisely to enable the working class to recognise its own relative cultural impoverishment and expropriation. Such work should aim at arousing an anger at this cultural expropriation, so it wants radically to change things – take back a culture which is, after all, built from its own surplus labour. The working class will never make a revolution unless it is conscious of its own unsatisfied needs.

Obviously in the case of the Soviet Union, as well as in Britain in 1977, there are three preconditions for the full realisation of the process of cultural access – a crucial element in any genuine liberation. Firstly, there is the political precondition, the transformation of the productive relations and the social relations obtaining in, for example, education. This will inevitably involve the conquest of state power which defends those ossified relations by the working class. This necessary, but insufficient, condition was obviously realised in Russia in 1917. Secondly, there is a particular pre-existing level of cultural development of the working class on which to build. Thirdly, there is the technological level of that particular society, especially the state of the 'communications'/media, which are precisely the modes of access or assimilation.

We must now examine the 'Proletcult debate' and the conclusions reached by its opponents in the light of the conditions of advanced, contemporary capitalist societies, such as Britain. For this purpose I shall be expounding and using many of the ideas of Hans Magnus Enzensberger, from his important essay 'Constituents of a Theory of the Media'.[7] I make no apology for borrowing those ideas – that is what ideas are for!

However, the first thing which should be established is what was meant by 'culture' in the context of the 1920s. We have already referred to Trotsky's working definition. This could be amended – 'culture' is an accumulated and coherent body of knowledge and technique, collectively held, from which to advance, both technologically and in any other field. But the main thing which needs to be emphasised is that in general the protagonists were principally talking of literature – a written culture. The literary mode was by far the most important form of communication and dissemination of culture at that time. Literacy, as an indispensable precondition of that process, was very limited.

Now, following certain ideas of Walter Benjamin, Enzensberger claims that written culture, and the heritage/tradition which it embodies, is 'class-specific'. What is implied here? Most people speak better than they write. Writing is a formalised technique and a process of social specialisation. Professional writers tend to think in caste terms. This is certainly true of journalists today, in my experience, despite the fact that they are quite obviously just one part of the productive process, like the printer, and the fact that many of their jobs, as specific entities, will rapidly become anachronistic in future years with the further penetration of electronic media technology.

The class character of a writer's work is undeniable. Apart from the content, the very form itself is one which precludes the mass of the population. This is not simply the result of capitalist economic control of the media. An 'ideological block' to writing is very strong in the working class. The reasons for this are not difficult to find. Intimidation through the written word has remained a widespread phenomenom, even in advanced industrial societies. This is reinforced by the very way that society transmits its writing techniques. For example, people learn to talk in psychologically favourable conditions, within the context of interaction in non-structured environments, amongst relatives, parents, friends. Writing, on the other hand, is generally learned within an authoritarian socialisation procedure, in the school. 'Good writing' is still seen as the equivalent of 'breaking in' in many schools, and the whole process of fluent writing and reading is regarded as a process of 'initiation' or 'admission' to a particular cultural heritage.

Within this socialisation process, the formalisation of written language encourages the repression of all opposition. Unresolved contradictions in speech betray themselves in pauses, hesitations, repetitions, slips, phrasing, expression and so on. The form of written culture scorns such involuntary factors as 'mistakes'. Written language demands the smoothing out of contradictions – the obsessive concern with spelling is the most prominent feature of this process in the junior school.

Similarly, the printed book – even this one – is a medium which operates as a monologue, isolating producer and consumer. Feedback and interaction are limited and the control circuit in the case of literary criticism is extremely cumbersome and elitist, excluding the mass of the public on principle.

None of the characteristics that distinguish written cultural forms *necessarily* apply to the modern electronic media. The microphone and the camera abolish the 'class-specific' character of the mode of production, though not, under capitalism, the actual productions themselves. As constituted, radio and television do exhibit authoritarian, limiting, undemocratic characteristics, but these are hangovers from an older, written culture – outworn characteristics demanded by the specific social relations. Such characteristics, however, go against the structure of those media, which demand interaction and accessibility. It is within this central contradiction, between the relations of capitalist control and the productive potentialities of those media, that socialists should intervene. Here is encapsulated the central contradiction of bourgeois society, in a specific form – that between the productive forces and the social relations which enchain them.

In this new situation the whole concept of culture, and its related concept, tradition, as embodied in an authoritarian, written form, is being broken down. Bourgeois culture is being threatened in a real sense. Only an archaic set of social relations hold back that liberating potential. From such an analysis, flow two conclusions.

1. One can understand why the petit-bourgeois intelligentsia, even on the left, has in general been hostile to these new media, often falling back on reactionary, romantic visions of such forms 'degrading' worthwhile artistic values and standards. Such new developments threaten that intelligentsia's priveleged positions, their *raison d'etre* within a literary, cultural tradition.

2. The importance in Britain of a political struggle by the workers' movement, against the state restriction on access to the electronic media, particularly radio and television. Such media could constitute massively liberating forces, in terms of organisational strength, the generalisation of socialist ideas and the assimilation of knowledge in all fields. We already have the precedent and experience of Italy to draw on – such a process has already begun there. These electronic, non-literary forms of media are obviously much better suited to the

proletariat's need to gain access to all forms of knowledge, independent of the class-specific written word, within the context of an inherently democratic, anti-authoritarian structure.

So, then, to reassess the Proletcult debate in the light of the British situation, we must go back to reconsider the three preconditions for proletarian access to bourgeois culture. Firstly, there is the primary political precondition, the conquest of the state apparatus and its replacement by proletarian organs of direct workers' democracy. But a struggle for that will at all times be shot through with elements of the cultural struggle to convince workers of their unsatisfied needs in this field. Central to this aspect of the politico-cultural struggle is the demand for 'free' radio and television, in place of the present paternalistic, restrictive, state-approved system.

The second factor which needs to be considered is the existing cultural level of the British proletariat, which is infinitely higher than that of the Russian masses, workers and peasants at the time of the Revolution. Literacy and numeracy is almost universal, with only an estimated 4 per cent of illiterates, compared with 80 per cent in the Russia of 1917. In addition, the problem of the peasantry as a disparate, potentially hostile component is non-existent. Much more of the prerequisites for running an industrial society – particularly technological knowledge – have been assimilated by significant sections of the proletariat. In addition, a large stratum of the intelligentsia in industry and other fields – the 'white-collar' sector – has been 'proletarianised' by the industrialisation processes of late capitalism. As such, firmly embedded as they are in the working class proper, such layers can act as very real 'transmitters' of vital bourgeois culture into wider and wider sections of the working class. This process if very important, because it seems partially to threaten the traditional Leninist notion of revolutionary ideas necessarily coming 'from the outside' – from a genuinely déclassé bourgeois and petit-bourgeois intelligentsia, separate from the working class proper. This process of the mass 'proletarianisation' of intellectual labour also impinges directly on the Gramscian notion of the 'organic intellectual', rooted in the working class, making such a concept more concrete and comprehensible.

The third factor is the technological precondition, which harks back to the ideas of Enzensberger elaborated earlier. Obviously in the Soviet Union the technological means of cultural dissemination were minimal – the printed word was primary and even the very paper on which it was printed was in chronic short supply.[8] Such a written form, in virtual isolation, provided a very cumbersome, authoritarian and inefficient form of disseminating culture, despite the fierce debates in the press, as described in Tariq Ali's contribution to this volume. Even the visual arts, then and now, were dependent on literary exposition and analysis for an informed, coherent understanding. Admittedly, theatre was also used to some extent and film crept in gradually throughout the 1920s, but these were fairly marginal forms in the context of an overwhelmingly written culture.

Today the massive technological means to non-written access to bourgeois culture are with us in abundance – radio, television, film, tape-recorders, cameras, video and a host of other electronic devices. As a result of the facility and universality of these forms – at present held back by the limitations of outmoded social relations demanded by bourgeois private ownership/control – steps towards the rapid assimilation of bourgeois knowledge and culture would be enormous in the modern conditions of a democratic workers' state. Given that this is the case, and given that the means of access to culture are already embryonically developed even within the framework of bourgeois society, one can see that the whole question of 'proletarian culture' takes on a whole new meaning and context.

Trotsky envisaged the creation of a new, non-derivative culture coinciding with the abolition of the dictatorship of the proletariat and the founding of a classless society. Until such time, the inheritance of the cultural gains of the past would be the principal priority. Only would that process be concluded with the assistance of revolution in the capitalist West. The Proletcult and their supporters, on the other hand, relied on the possibility of the creation of a new 'proletarian culture' during the period of the dictatorship of the proletariat, regardless of the cultural impoverishment of the Soviet Union and the lack of revolutions elsewhere. However, for Trotsky the whole political and social process would take a relatively short period (if aided by other revolutionary states). For the Proletcult, or at least their 'friends', Stalin, Bukharin and Lunacharsky, that process in isolation would necessarily take an enormous length of time – 'at a snail's pace', as Bukharin put it.

Today we can say that after revolutions in the industrialised West, the dictatorship of the proletariat would be faced with far fewer material barriers to its own self-abolition as a distinct class, depending on the resistance of the bourgeoisie internally and in those countries where it had still not been overthrown. But a crucial part of that process, the assimilation of pre-existing bourgeois culture, given the means at the working class's disposal, would take a very short period of time indeed. It is possible that these developments could lead to the early assertion of qualitatively new cultural forms, unforeseen by us today, which clearly transcend their bourgeois heritage. Whether one calls such forms 'proletarian' seems immaterial, providing one recognises that it is the conditions of the different social formation which could make such innovations rapidly possible. *In any case, any element of 'prescription' would be unthinkable.* The problem arose in the Soviet Union because of the low level of resources available – with the obvious related necessity to select, choose and make priorities. Within that situation the Proletcult tried unsuccessfully to claim preferential treatment. With the abundance of media resources carried over from an advanced capitalist society, such a dangerously restrictive necessity will probably not arise.

Two additional points compound this provisional hypothesis. Firstly, an important task of the 'dictatorship of the proletariat' will be the defeat of the bourgeoisie on the ideological terrain. This will principally be achieved in and through the media. The needs of the dictatorship would seem to imply the necessity for the rapid development of proletarian forms of 'culture as combat' against the strongly entrenched bourgeois tradition – assimilation and negation will take place side by side. In the Soviet Union on the other hand, the principal forms of ideology which needed combating were not bourgeois but pre-capitalist – that is, feudal and medieval. For such purposes the written word, limited as it no doubt was, was adequate and was in fact itself a revolutionary form in those conditions.

Secondly, through the work of structuralism and semiology, particularly in television and film, there is an increasing recognition that media are not just simply transmitters – modes of consumption – of meanings, but are themselves generators – modes of production – of meanings. The implication of this would seem to be that, rapidly within the media in a post-capitalist society, the mere transmission of prior culture using a passive, 'transparent' view of the functions of the media will be superseded by the necessity to turn such media into active generators of new forms and meanings which transcend the ideological limitations of previous forms and techniques. This kind of development would necessarily be a radical challenge to accepted notions of media as mere 'reflectors' of pre-existent forms of culture.

The final implication of this overall analysis, which Enzensberger shares, is that we can envisage the end of written culture within a socialist society. The main forms of culture which would be developed in such a society would be non-literary, particularly electronic and audio-visual. Poetry and painting, as presently constituted, could therefore be superseded. This is not to say that they would cease to exist, but they would become marginal cases within a much broader theory and practice. This has already happened with painting, *vis-à-vis* film and photography. We cannot use the criteria of the former to assess the latter (though many pedants still try) but a larger 'aesthetic' is needed to encompass the former as a special, minor case.

Notes on the Contributors

The Editor

CARL GARDNER was born in Manchester in 1948. After graduating in philosophy from Exeter University in 1969, he did a host of jobs from selling ice-cream to brushing factory floors. After training as a teacher in further education he found his way, purely by chance, into the media. He worked for three years as designer, journalist and production worker on the newspaper *Red Weekly* and then three years ago moved on to the London weekly magazine *Time Out* as a production journalist. He now writes on television for the same journal. He is an active and militant member of the National Union of Journalists and has contributed regularly to its newspaper. He was a founder member of both the Campaign Against Racism in the Media and the quarterly left-wing cultural magazine *Wedge*. He has written regularly on political and cultural questions for *Red Weekly* and its successor *Socialist Challenge*. He is at present researching a study of the treatment of science by television.

The Contributors

TARIQ ALI was born in Lahore, Pakistan, in 1943. After graduating from Oxford University in 1965 he worked for a period as the theatre critic and reviews editor for *Town* magazine (now defunct). He visited

Cambodia and North Vietnam for the Bertrand Russell War Crimes Tribunal in 1967 and helped to establish the Vietnam Solidarity Campaign in the same year. Since 1968 he has been a leading militant of the Fourth International and its British affiliate, the International Marxist Group. He helped to found the journals *Black Dwarf* and *Red Mole* and edited both for a period. He is the author of a number of books and pamphlets on subjects as wide-ranging as Pakistan, Britain and Chile. Since June 1977 he has been editor of the left-wing weekly *Socialist Challenge* and recently published a book on *1968 and After*.

DAVE BAILEY is a leading member of the International Marxist Group and worked on its newspaper, *Red Weekly*, for two years as a journalist. He is the author of several IMG publications on such diverse issues as nationalisation, education and racism. He worked in print production for two years and is at present researching a study of the European revolution.

DAVID GLYN has been an independent film-maker for a number of years. He is a member of the executive of the Independent Film-makers Association and worked for some time for the Other Cinema. He has contributed to the film magazine *AfterImage* and recently made a film about South Africa, *Namibia Armed*.

GARY HERMAN is a freelance writer and sometime contributor to the music press in Britain, the United States and Germany. He is author of *The Who* and has been responsible for a number of other books on diverse aspects of politics and culture in the post-war world. Formerly a member of the IS (now the Socialist Workers' Party) he retains a firm commitment to revolutionary politics.

IAN HOARE is a member of the National Union of Journalists who has worked in radio, television, magazines and books. He belonged to the now defunct Rock Writers' Cooperative, and is co-author and editor of *The Soul Book*. He was active in the Music for Socialism organisation and has been a member of the *Wedge* editorial collective.

CLAIRE JOHNSTON is a lecturer in film studies and a member of the *Screen* magazine editorial board. She is the organiser of the special events at the Edinburgh Film Festival. She has worked for a number of years as a film-maker and film theorist in the women's film movement.

MANDY MERCK helped to organise the 'Women in the Communications Industries' conference held in London in 1975. She has contributed to *Red Rag, Spare Rib* and *Women's Report* magazines and was a founder-member of the *Wedge* editorial collective. She currently works for *Time Out*.

ROGER PROTZ has been a journalist for more than twenty years. He edited *Keep Left* in the early 1960s and *Socialist Worker* from 1968 to 1974. He has worked for the London *Evening Standard* and *New Society* and has also lectured in journalism. He is now editor of publications with the Campaign for Real Ale, the radical consumer movement, and is an active member of the National Union of Journalists.

CHRIS RAWLENCE was born in 1945. He lives in Leeds and is a founder-member of Red Ladder Theatre. He has worked with the company since 1968 as a performer, writer, administrator, designer and director. He is also an art historian and taught art history at the Slade School of Fine Art, University College, from 1969 to 1973.

LEON ROSSELSON is a socialist singer–songwriter. He has been a radical figure in popular music since the early 1960s, when he contributed several satirical songs to the television programme *That Was The Week That Was*. He has written and performed all over Britain for folk audiences, and has written three plays for the fringe and radio. He worked for two years for Inter-Action's Dogg's Troupe and the Fun Art Bus, writing scripts and songs. His songs have appeared in many publications, including *Tribune, Fireweed, Folk Review* and the *Big Red Song Book*, as well as in two of his own song collections. He has made several LPs, both solo and with Roy Bailey, including *Palaces of Gold, That's Not the Way It's Got to Be* and *Love, Loneliness and Laundry*. One of his recent songs, 'Talking Grunwick', forms part of the sound-track of Newsreel Collective's film *Stand Together*.

GEOFFREY SHERIDAN is presently on the staff of *Socialist Challenge*. As a freelance journalist for seven years he was a regular contributor to a number of national magazines and newspapers, including the *Guardian*, where he was chairperson of the *Guardian* Freelance Group. He is a recent member of the National Union of Journalists' Freelance Industrial Council, and former secretary of the Campaign Against Racism in the Media.

GILLIAN SKIRROW is a lecturer/producer at the Centre for Educational Practice, University of Strathclyde. She was an education officer with Thames Television for three years and a teacher for many years before that. She is a recent contributor to *Screen* magazine.

JOHN THACKARA is a commissioning editor in publishing. He is active in the National Union of Journalists and a founder-member and present secretary of the Campaign Against Racism in the Media.

RAYMOND WILLIAMS was born in Wales in 1921 and educated at Trinity College, Cambridge. In 1967 he was elected a Fellow of Jesus College, Cambridge, where he is a lecturer in English. To date, he is probably the most prominent and wide-ranging writer and theorist on the British left on questions of culture and the media. He is author of *Culture and Society, 1780–1950* (1958), *The Long Revolution* (1961), *Communications* (1966), *The Country and the City* (1973), *Television: Technology and Cultural Form* (1974), *Keywords* (1976) and *Marxism and Literature* (1977).

Notes and References

Introduction

1. *New Left Review*, no. 82.
2. Raymond Williams, *Marxism and Literature* (Oxford University Press, 1977).
3. *New Left Review*, nos 95, 99.
4. *New Left Review*, no. 99, p. 56.
5. Ibid., p. 60.
6. David Glyn, 'A reply to Williams', *Wedge*, no. 1.
7. Ibid., p. 38.
8. For a discussion of the film *Riddles of the Sphinx* with Laura Mulvey, see *Wedge*, no. 2.
9. Ernest Fischer, *The Necessity of Art* (Harmondsworth: Penguin, 1970).
10. 'The Political Theatre', *New Edinburgh Review*, no. 30.
11. 'Grant Aid and Political Theatre 1968–77', *Wedge*, nos 1, 2.

Chapter 1

1. A slightly different version of this article first appeared in *International*, vol. 3, no. 3, and was reprinted in *Wedge*, no. 1.
2. Raymond Williams, *The Long Revolution* (Harmondsworth: Penguin, 1965).
3. In Richard Boston (ed.), *The Press We Deserve* (London: Routledge and Kegan Paul, 1970).

Chapter 2

1. *Times Higher Education Supplement*, 7 October 1977.

2. Ibid., 19 November 1976.

3. Independent Broadcasting Authority Act, 1973, chapter 19, section 4.

4. Guidance note for directors of programme companies, IBA, August 1976.

5. ITV primary topic chart for 1978–9 in *ITCA*, 1978.

6. Stuart Hall, Ian Connell and Lidia Curtis, 'The Unity of Current Affairs Television', *Working Papers in Cultural Studies* (WPCS) no. 9, spring 1976.

7. See, for example, S. Heath and G. Skirrow, 'Television: a World in Action', *Screen*, vol. 18, no. 2.

8. The full text is given in *Screen Education*, no. 19, summer 1976.

9. Glasgow University Media Group, *Bad News* (London: Routledge and Kegan Paul, 1976).

Chapter 3

1. See Anthony Scaduto, *Bob Dylan* (London: Abacus, 1972) p. 218.

2. See R. Serge Denisoff, *Great Day Coming* (University of Illinois, 1972) p. 124.

3. Quoted in Sy and Barbara Ribakove, *Folk Rock: The Bob Dylan Story* (New York, 1966).

4. See Tony Palmer, *Born Under a Bad Sign* (London: William Kimber, 1970) p. 149.

5. *Melody Maker*, 26 February 1977.

6. A. L. Lloyd, *Folk Song in England* (London: Panther, 1975).

Chapter 4

1. Hans Magnus Enzensberger, 'Constituents of a Theory of the Media', in *Raids and Reconstructions* (London: Pluto, 1976) p. 53.

2. See Karl Marx, *Theories of Surplus Value*, part 1 (Moscow: Progress Publishers, 1975) for Marx's discussion on 'capitalism and spiritual production'.

3. Walter Benjamin, 'The Work of Art in the Age of Mechanical Reproduction', in *Illuminations* (London: Collins/Fontana, 1973) p. 229.

4. See William Morris, 'Art and Labour', in *The Political Writings of William Morris* (New York: International Publishers, 1968).

5. See A. L. Lloyd, *Folk Song in England* (London: Panther, 1975).

6. See Trevor Fisher, *We're Only in it for the Money*, (pamphlet reprinted by Chris Whitbread, Hackney Music Workshop, 1975).

7. Enzensberger, 'Constituents of a Theory of the Media', p. 27.

8. Leon Trotsky, 'Culture and Socialism', in *Culture and Socialism and a Manifesto: Art and Revolution* (London: New Park Publications, 1975) p. 24.

9. Leon Trotsky and André Breton, 'Art and Revolution' in *Culture and Socialism and a Manifesto: Art and Revolution*, p. 33.

10. Antonio Gramsci, *Prison Notebooks* (London: Lawrence and Wishart, 1971) p. 433.

11. Dave Laing, 'Brecht's Theatre Poems: an Introduction', *Wedge*, no. 1, p. 56.

Chapter 5

1. Raymond Williams, *Culture and Society, 1780–1950* (Harmondsworth: Penguin, 1971).

Chapter 6

1. I am concentrating here on the situation of a particular section of film-makers – broadly, those in and around the Independent Film-makers' Association (IFA). There are certainly others who designate themselves 'independent' but I shall argue that the political perspectives of these are fundamentally tied to the capitalist industry as such. Insofar as this is the case, this group is less central to the argument of the present article. That argument is that in the film industry, if in no other, we presently face the concrete alternative: socialism or barbarism.

2. Draft paper for the 1977 annual general meeting of the IFA produced by London Region ACTT Working Party, p. 2.

3. *The Future of the British Film Industry: Report of the Prime Minister's Working Party* – the Terry Report (London: HMSO, 1976) Cmnd. 6372; *Proposals for the Setting up of a British Film Authority: Report of the Interim Action Committee on the Film Industry* – the Wilson Committee Report (London: HMSO, 1978) Cmnd. 7071.

Chapter 7

1. Terry Eagleton, *Criticism and Ideology* (London: New Left Books, 1977).

2. Walter Benjamin, 'The Work of Art in the Age of Mechanical Reproduction' in *Illuminations* (London: Collins/Fontana, 1973).

3. See especially Robin Wood, *Hitchcock's Films*, revised edn (London: Tantivy Press, 1977).

4. Peter Wollen, *Signs and Meaning in the Cinema* (London: Secker and Warburg, 1968).

5. *Edinburgh '76 Magazine* (London: BFI, 1976).

6. Hans Magnus Enzensberger, 'Constituents of a Theory of the Media', in *Raids and Reconstructions* (London: Pluto, 1976).

Chapter 9

1. The complete McGraw-Hill guidelines are reprinted in *Sexism in Children's Books*, edited by the Children's Rights Workshop (London: Writers' and Readers' Publishing Co-operative, 1976) pp. 44–56.

2. Josephine King and Mary Stott (eds), *Is This Your Life? Images of Women in the Media* (London: Virago, 1977) p. 2.

3. Celia Pugh, 'Why 51 Per Cent of the Population Can't Be Kept in their Place', *Socialist Challenge*, 26 January 1978, p. 7.

4. Vicki McKenzie, 'Boobed Again!', *Observer*, 5 February 1978, p. 22.

5. Ellen Willis, 'The Conservatism of Ms.' in *Feminist Revolution* (New York: New Paltz, 1975) pp. 173–4.

6. Elena Lieven, 'Patriarchy', *Red Shift*, Feminist Issue, 1977, p. 8.

7. Ibid.

8. Ibid.

9. From the *Times Literary Supplement*, 12 October 1973, as cited in *Edinburgh '76 Magazine* (London: BFI, 1976) p. 4.

10. Cf. Juliet Mitchell, *Psychoanalysis and Feminism* (London: Allen Lane, 1974) especially pp. 382–98.

11. Louis Althusser, 'Freud and Lacan' in *Lenin and Philosophy* (New York: Monthly Review Press, 1971) pp. 201–10.

12. King and Stott (eds), *Is This Your Life? Images of Women in the Media*, p. 19.

13. Ibid., p. 43.

14. Ibid., pp. 74–5.

15. Ibid., pp. 93–4.

16. For an analysis of such variations, see John Goode, 'Women and the Literary Text' Juliet Mitchell and Ann Oakley (eds), *The Rights and Wrongs of Women* (Harmondsworth: Penguin, 1976) pp. 217–55.

17. King and Stott (eds), *Is This Your Life? Images of Women in the Media*, p. 119.

18. Laura Mulvey, 'Visual Pleasure and Narrative Cinema', *Screen*, autumn 1975, p. 11.

19. Ibid., pp. 12–13.

20. Ibid., p. 17.

21. For a detailed analysis of the presentation of women in newspapers, see Helen Butcher, Ros Coward, Marcelle Evaristi, Jenny Garber, Rachel Harrison and Janice Winship, *Images of Women in the Media* (Stencilled Occasional Papers, Centre for Contemporary Cultural Studies, University of Birmingham, 1974).

22. Virginia Woolf, *A Room of One's Own* (Harmondsworth: Penguin, 1963) p. 35.

23. *Images of Women: Guidelines for Promoting Equality through Journalism* (London: National Union of Journalists Equality Working Party, 1977).

Chapter 10

1. Peter Evans, *Publish and Be Damned!* (London: Runnymede Trust, 1976).

Chapter 11

1. The phrase 'press freedom' and the word 'press' should be taken to refer to newspapers, radio and television throughout the chapter, unless otherwise specified.

2. Hans Magnus Enzensberger, 'Industrialisation of the Mind' in *Raids and Reconstructions* (London: Pluto, 1976) pp. 14–16.

3. Andrew Goodman, 'Working in Television – the Experience of Censorship and Control', in Peter Beharrell and Greg Philo (eds), *Trade Unions and the Media* (London: Macmillan, 1977).

4. John Whale, *The Politics of the Media* (London: Fontana, 1977).

5. Glasgow University Media Group, *Bad News* (London: Routledge and Kegan Paul, 1976).

6. *In Black and White: Racist Reporting and How to Fight It* (CARM pamphlet, 1977).

7. For a fuller summary, see Beharrell and Philo (eds), *Trade Unions and the Media*, chs 9, 10.

8. See John Thackara's essay in this volume for a fuller discussion of this question.

9. The full NUJ code of conduct is reprinted as an appendix in Peter Evans, *In Black and White* and in Beharrell and Philo (eds), *Trade Unions and the Media*.

10. Hans Magnus Enzensberger, 'Constituents of a Theory of the Media' in *Raids and Reconstructions* (London: Pluto, 1976) p. 41.

Chapter 12

1. *Nationalising the Film Industry* – report of the ACTT Nationalisation Forum (ACTT publication, 1973).

2. Marshall McLuhan, *Understanding Media* (London: Sphere Books, 1967).

3. Hans Magnus Enzensberger, 'Constituents of a Theory of the Media', in *Raids and Reconstructions* (London: Pluto, 1976).

4. V. I. Lenin, 'The Impending Catastrophe and How to Combat it', in *Selected Works*, vol. 2 (London: Lawrence and Wishart, 1964). Also Leon Trotsky, *The Struggle Against Fascism in Germany* (New York: Pathfinder, 1971).

5. Ernest Mandel, 'Self-Management: Dangers and Possibilities', *International*, vol. 3, no. 3.

Chapter 13

1. Sheila Fitzpatrick, *The Commissariat of the Enlightenment* (Cambridge University Press, 1970) p. 14.

2. Leon Trotsky, Diego Rivera and André Breton, 'Manifesto for an Independent Revolutionary Art', reprinted in André Breton, *What is Surrealism?* (London: Pluto Press, 1978) p. 185.

3. See Victor Serge, *Year One of the Russian Revolution* (London: Allen Lane, 1972).

4. D. Stermer, *The Art of Revolution* (London: Pall Mall, 1970).

5. See M. Grimshaw and C. Gardner, 'Free Radio in Italy', *Wedge*, no. 1.

6. A very important contribution in this respect is the statement by the United Secretariat of the Fourth International, 'Socialist Democracy and the Dictatorship of the Proletariat', *Inprecor*, 7 July 1977.

Chapter 14

1. John Berger, *A Painter of Our Time* (London: Writers' and Readers' Publishing Co-operative, 1976) p. 76.

2. Leon Trotsky, *Literature and Revolution* (Ann Arbor Press, 1960), p. 14.

3. Ibid., pp. 190–1.

4. Zhadnov was Stalin's henchman in the cultural field in the 1930s.

5. Trotsky, *Literature and Revolution*, p. 218.

6. Ibid., p. 191.

7. Hans Magnus Enzensberger, 'Constituents of a Theory of the Media', in *Raids and Reconstructions* (London: Pluto, 1976).

8. Ironically it seems that this particular shortcoming has still not been overcome, with paper shortages in the present-day Soviet Union being regular events. This, in an epoch when Soviet scientists can bounce messages off the moon, brings home quite clearly the degree to which even post-capitalist states are still liable to the vicious exigencies of the law of combined and uneven development.

Bibliography

The books and articles selected for inclusion have been recommended by the contributors as useful background material to the areas covered in the various essays. Also included are the most important of the references mentioned by the contributors.

General

Hans Magnus Enzensberger, 'Constituents of a Theory of the Media', in *Raids and Reconstructions* (London: Pluto, 1976).

Hans Magnus Enzensberger, 'Industrialisation of the Mind', in *Raids and Reconstructions* (London: Pluto, 1976).

Walter Benjamin, 'The Work of Art in the Age of Mechanical Reproduction', in *Illuminations* (London: Collins/Fontana, 1973).

Walter Benjamin, 'The Author as Producer', *New Left Review*, no. 62

Raymond Williams, *Culture and Society, 1780–1950* (Harmondsworth: Penguin, 1971).

Raymond Williams, *The Long Revolution* (Harmondsworth: Penguin, 1965).

Leon Trotsky, *Literature and Revolution* (Ann Arbor Press, 1960).

Leon Trotsky, *On Literature and Art* (New York: Pathfinder, 1970).

G. Murdock and P. Golding, 'For a Political Economy of Mass

Communications', in R. Miliband and J. Saville (eds), *Socialist Register* (London: Merlin Press, 1973).

R. Coward and J. Ellis, *Language and Materialism* (London: Routledge and Kegan Paul, 1977).

Roland Barthes, *Elements of Semiology* (London: Cape, 1967).

Perry Anderson, 'Components of a National Culture', in A. Cockburn and R. Blackburn (eds), *Student Power* (Harmondsworth: Penguin, 1970).

S. Hall and P. Whannell, *The Popular Arts* (London: Hutchinson, 1964).

M. Vicinus, *The Industrial Muse* (London: Croom Helm, 1974).

Marxism and the Mass Media: towards a basic bibilography (Paris and New York: International Mass Media Research Centre, 1976).

Theodor Adorno and Max Horkheimer, 'The Culture Industry: Enlightenment as Mass Deception', in *Dialectic of Enlightenment* (London: Allen Lane, 1973).

Marxist Readings: a Bibliography (Bagnolet: Critiques Livres, 1977; distributed by Journeyman Press, London).

Terry Eagleton, *Criticism and Ideology* (London: New Left Books, 1977).

Terry Eagleton, 'Criticism and Politics: the Work of Raymond Williams', *New Left Review*, no. 95.

Anthony Barnett, 'Raymond Williams and Marxism: a Rejoinder to Eagleton', *New Left Review*, no. 99.

Music

H. Stuckenschmidt, *Twentieth Century Music* (London: Weidenfeld and Nicolson, 1969).

Frank Kovsky, *Black Nationalism and the Revolution in Music* (New York: Pathfinder, 1970).

Theodor Adorno, *Philosophy of Modern Music* (London: Sheed and Ward, 1973).

Hans Eisler (with Theodor Adorno), *Composing for the Films* (New York: Oxford University Press, 1947).

Roland Barthes, *Image–Music–Text* (London: Fontana, 1977).

William Weber, *Music and the Middle Class* (London: Croom Helm, 1975).

A. Peacock and R. Weir, *The Composer in the Market Place*, (London: Faber, 1975).

E. D. Mackerness, *The Social History of English Music* (London: Routledge and Kegan Paul, 1975).
A. L. Lloyd, *Folk Song in England* (London: Panther, 1975).

Theatre

J. Willett (ed.), *Brecht on Theatre* (London: Methuen, 1964).
E. Braun (ed.), *Meyerhold on Theatre* (London: Methuen, 1969).
New Edinburgh Review, no. 30, *The Political Theatre*.
Bruce Birchall, 'Grant Aid and Political Theatre, 1968–77', *Wedge*, nos. 1, 2.
Dave Laing, 'Brecht's Theatre Poems', *Wedge*, no. 1.

Cinema

Peter Wollen, *Signs and Meanings in the Cinema* (London: Secker and Warburg, 1968).
Peter Wollen, 'The Two Avant-Gardes' *Edinburgh '76 Magazine* (London: BFI, 1976).
Edinburgh '76 Magazine (London: BFI, 1976).
Edinburgh '77 Magazine (London: BFI, 1977).
Laura Mulvey, 'Visual Pleasure and Narrative Cinema', *Screen*, autumn 1975.
Joan Mellen, *Women and Their Sexuality in the New Film* (London: Davis-Poynter, 1974).
Nationalising the Film Industry (ACTT publication, 1973).
Notes on Women's Cinema (SEFT publication, 1973).
Michael Chanan, *Labour Power in the British Film Industry* (London: BFI, 1976).
AfterImage, no. 6, 1976, *Perspectives on English Independent Cinema*.
J. Spraos, *The Decline of the Cinema* (London: Allen and Unwin, 1962).
T. Kelly, *A Competitive Cinema* (London: Institute of Economic Affairs, 1966).
T. Guback, *The International Film Industry* (Indiana University Press, 1969).
D. Macpherson (ed.), *Independent Cinema in the 30s* (London: BFI, 1978).

Racism in the Media

Charles Husband (ed.), *White Media, Black Britain* (London: Arrow, 1975).

In Black and White: Racist Reporting and How to Fight It (Campaign Against Racism in the Media pamphlet, 1977).

Peter Evans, *Publish and Be Damned!* (London: Runnymede Trust, 1976).

Dave Bailey, *The Socialist Challenge to Racism* (*Red Weekly* pamphlet, 1977).

Sexism in the Media

J. King and M. Stott (eds), *Is This Your Life? Images of Women in the Media* (London: Virago, 1977).

C. Adams and R. Laurikeitis, *The Gender Trap*, Book 3, *Messages and Images* (London: Quartet, 1976).

Images of Women (NUJ pamphlet, 1975).

Sue Sharpe, *Just Like a Girl* (Harmondsworth: Penguin, 1976).

Joan Mellen, *Women and Their Sexuality in the New Film* (London: Davis-Poynter, 1974).

R. Coward *et al.*, *Images of Women in the Media* (Stencilled Occasional Papers, Centre for Contemporary Cultural Studies, University of Birmingham, 1974).

Press, Television and Radio

Raymond Williams, *Communications* (Harmondsworth: Penguin, 1970).

Raymond Williams, *Television: Technology and Cultural Form* (London: Fontana, 1974).

Glasgow University Media Group, *Bad News* (London: Routledge and Kegan Paul, 1976).

Peter Beharrell and Greg Philo (eds), *Trade Unions and The Media* (London: Macmillan, 1977).

S. Heath and G. Skirrow, 'Television: World in Action', *Screen*, Vol. 18, no. 2.

M. Grimshaw and C. Gardner, 'Free Radio in Italy', *Wedge*, no. 1.

John Whale, *The Politics of the Media* (London: Fontana, 1977).

John Whale, *The Half-Shut Eye: Television and Politics in Britain and America* (London: Macmillan, 1969).

Armand Mattelart, *Multinationals and Communications Systems: the Ideological Apparatus of Imperialism* (Hassocks: Harvester Press, 1978).

TV Handbook (Free Communications Group publication, 1973).

Cultural Studies No 9 (Centre for Contemporary Cultural Studies, University of Birmingham, 1976).

Nicholas Garnham, *Structures of Television* (London: BFI, 1976).

Paul Hoch, *The Newspaper Game* (London: Calder and Boyars, 1974).

Alan J. Lee, *The Origins of the Popular Press* (London: Croom Helm, 1976).

Stanley Harrison, *Poor Man's Guardian* (London: Lawrence and Wishart, 1974).

Jeremy Tunstall, *The Media Are American* (London: Constable, 1977).

Herbert Brucker, *Communication is Power* (New York: Oxford University Press, 1973).

Richard Collins, *Television News* (London: BFI, 1976).

The Media, Workers' Control and Socialist Democracy

United Secretariat of the Fourth International, statement, 'Socialist Democracy and the Dictatorship of the Proletariat', *Inprecor*, 7 July 1977.

Nationalising the Film Industry (ACTT publication, 1973).

D. Stermer, *The Art of Revolution* (London: Pall Mall, 1970).

Index